THE FORMATION OF THE BIBLE

Are Any Books Missing?

G. Michael Cocoris

© 2012, 2025 by G. Michael Cocoris

All rights reserved. This publication may not be reproduced (in whole or in part, edited, or revised) in any way, form, or means, including, but not limited to electronic, mechanical, photocopying, recording or any kind of storage and retrieval system *for sale*, except for brief quotations in printed reviews, without the written permission of G. Michael Cocoris, 2016 Euclid #20, Santa Monica, CA 90405, michaelcocoris@gmail.com, or his appointed representatives. Permission is hereby granted, however, for the reproduction of the whole or parts of the whole without changing the content in any way for *free distribution*, provided all copies contain this copyright notice in its entirety. Permission is also granted to charge for the cost of copying.

Unless otherwise indicated, all Scripture quotations are taken from the New King James Version ®, Copyright © 1979, 1980, 1982 by Thomas Nelson, Inc. Used by permission. All rights reserved.

Cover design by John and Mike Cocoris
Interior design by John Cocoris

TABLE OF CONTENTS

Preface

Chapter

   1 Introduction   1

   2 The Formation of The Old Testament   11

   3 The Final Formation of The Old Testament   27

   4 Formal Recognition of The Old Testament   33

   5 The Debate About The Old Testament   43

   6 The Formation of The New Testament   49

   7 Recognition In The Early Church   59

   8 The Debate About The New Testament   93

   9 Formal Recognition of The New Testament   109

  10 Conclusion   113

Appendix   123

Bibliography   125

About The Author   129

Chapter 1

INTRODUCTION

How was the Bible put together? Who determined which books to include and which books to exclude? Are there books in the Bible that should not be there? Are there "lost books" of the Bible that ought to be in the Bible but, for some reason, did not make it? Before answering those questions, several preliminary issues need to be addressed.

Terms

As in any field, the place to begin is the definition of terms. In the case of the formation of the Bible, the terms that need clarification are revelation, inspiration, and canonization.

Revelation From a theological point of view, "revelation" is the *giving* of truth. God has revealed the truth about Himself, people, salvation, etc. Not all revelation has been recorded. Paul writes, "I will come to visions and revelations of the Lord: I know a man in Christ who fourteen years ago; whether in the body I do not know, or whether out of the body, I do not know, God knows; such a one was caught up to the third heaven. And I know such a man; whether in the body or out of the body I do not know, God knows; how he was caught up into Paradise and heard inexpressible words, which it is not lawful for a man to utter" (2 Cor. 12:1-4). God gave revelations that the recipient was not allowed to utter, much less write.

Inspiration Whereas revelation is the *giving* of truth, inspiration is the *recording* of truth. Peter explains that Scripture did not originate with men (2 Pet. 1:20), but holy men of God were "moved by the Holy Spirit" (2 Pet. 1:21). God influenced the human authors of Scripture so that what they wrote was the Word of God (Erickson, p. 199).

As there can be revelation without inspiration, there can also be inspiration without revelation. Inspiration is the *recording* of truth from *whatever* source it was obtained. The writers of Scripture recorded direct revelation, as in the case of the Ten Commandments, but they also recorded truth from their experience (Joshua), from research (Lk. 1:1-4), and even from written sources outside the Bible (Titus 1:12). In other words, to say that the Bible is inspired of God does not mean that God *directly* revealed everything in the Bible to men. Instead, it means that regardless of the source of their information, the Holy Spirit directed them so that what they wrote was what God intended for them to record in His Word.

Canonization The English word "canon" comes from a Greek word that originally meant "rod, bar, measuring rule," hence, "a rule or standard." It is used in Galatians as the standard by which believers are to measure their lives. Paul says, "As many as walk according to this rule, peace and mercy *be* upon them, and upon the Israel of God" (Gal. 6:16). Eventually, the term "canon" came to be used for a *collection* of books that met the standard of being the Word of God. Origen (A.D. 185-254) speaks of the "canonized Scriptures" (commentary on Mt., sec. 28) and Athanasius (ca. A.D. 293-373) of the "books which have been canonized" (Athanasius, *Easter Letter*, A.D. 367). In other words, "canon" came to be applied to the books that "conform to the rule or standard of divine inspiration" (Archer, p. 59). In this sense, "canon" is another word for "Bible." To be a bit more precise, the term "canon" is used for "a *closed* collection of books inspired by the Spirit of God" (R. K. Harrison, p. 262, italics added).

The Bible was written over about fifteen hundred years. The process began with Moses; later, other books were added to the canon. Therefore, the questions in forming the Bible are: "When were the additional books added? Who decides what books should be part of the collection of inspired books? When was the collection of inspired books (the canon) closed?" The ultimate issue is, "When was the canon *closed*?

Problems

There are several problems connected with determining when the canon was closed.

Information Neither the Bible nor extra-biblical sources give much information about the formation of the Bible. The available evidence has been described as "very sketchy and inferential in nature" (McDonald, p. 4). Noting the incompleteness of the information in the extant early Christian literature, Zahn observed that in early church history, the formation of the Bible was never at any time became the "object of serious dogmatic thinking or of real doctrinal formation" (Zahn, cited by Campenhausen, p. ix).

To say there is not *much* information does not mean there is *no* information. There is some data.

Interpretations Another difficulty is interpreting the available information. Several theories have been proposed, and, as expected, there is "little agreement among scholars" (McDonald, p. 18). Campenhausen says, "Everyone knows how scanty are our extant sources for the first, crucial centuries in particular, and how easily they tempt one to fill the gaps with more or less fantastic hypotheses or to overstrain the little evidence we have by violent interpretation."

In sorting through the various theories, it should be remembered that all theories are based on presuppositions. The theories of the formation of the Bible are no different. One of the questions that needs to be answered is, "What is the premise on which a particular theory of the formation of the Bible is based?"

What are the theories of the formation of the Bible?

Theories

The Traditional Position The traditional view is that since God inspired the Word, He made sure it was recognized, collected, preserved, and used. Bruce says, "The historic Christian belief is that the Holy Spirit, who controlled the writing of the individual books, also controlled their selection and collection, thus continuing to fulfill our Lord's promise that He would guide His disciples into all the truth. This, however, is something that is to be discerned by spiritual insight and not by historical research" (Bruce, *The New Testament Documents Are They Reliable?* p. 21). When Paul wrote, "All Scripture is given by inspiration of God" (2 Tim. 3:16), he had the Old Testament (1 Tim. 3:17) and the New Testament (1 Tim. 5:18) in mind. Surely, if God is the Author of all Scripture, He providentially provided for it to be recognized, preserved, and used. Jesus said that both the Law and His Word would be permanently preserved. In His Sermon on the Mount, He said, "For assuredly, I say to you, till heaven and earth pass away, one jot or one tittle will by no means pass from the law till all is fulfilled" (Mt. 5:18). Concerning His own words, Jesus said, "Heaven and earth will pass away, but My words will by no means pass away" (Mt. 24:35; see also Mk. 13:31; Lk. 21:33).

For variations within the Evangelical position, see "Evangelicals and the Canon of the New Testament" by M. James Sawyer. Sawyer concludes that the risen Christ "causes His church to accept the canon and to recognize it by means of the witness of the Spirit" (Sawyer, p. 47).

The Historical Approach The historical position begins with history. McDonald declares, "Since the origin of the biblical canon is a historical question, it seems the only defensible position is one that can be historically coherent and can best account for the surviving traditions in the church" (McDonald, p. 438). He builds his massive, 549-page tome concerning the canon on the assumption that "What we cannot show, we do not know," a quotation from Jacob Neusner (McDonald, pp. xv-xvi). According to this approach, all we know about canonicity is what we can glean from ancient sources (McDonald, p. xxxii).

As pointed out, the information from ancient sources is very sketchy. The canon was not discussed in the writings that have survived from the early years of church history. Nevertheless, based on historical data, numerous theories have been proposed.

For example, the first specific mention of a New Testament canon in church history was Marcion's canon (AD 140), which consisted of the Gospel of Luke and ten of the epistles of Paul. Campenhausen contends that the idea of a new collection of Scripture is nowhere to be found until the "idea came into existence at one stroke with Marcion and only with Marcion" (Campenhausen, p. 148). Others argue that there is evidence for a canon before Marcion (for example, Unnik, cited by Everett Harrison and Harrison himself; see Harrison, pp. 108-109).

Harnack proposed that the New Testament canon was developed as a reaction to Marcion. There is no question that there was a reaction to Marcion's restricted canon, but that does not mean there was no canon before Marcion. On the contrary, there are indications of a recognized canon before Marcion. Besides, the fact that Christians rejected Macron's canon indicated that they had a canon, and his canon did not match up to it! Scholars no longer accept Harnack's theory.

Goodspeed "approaches the study of the canon largely from the standpoint of the historian" and "dubiously employs the precarious argument from silence" (Everett Harrison, p. 110).

Introduction

Assuming the canon is a historical question (an assumption that can be questioned) and that what cannot be shown cannot be known, McDonald concludes that the canonization of the Old Testament "was not complete until the fourth or fifth centuries for most of Christendom" (McDonald, p. xvi). He says something similar about the New Testament canon (McDonald, p. 438). He insists on not concluding the canon until we have a record of someone *naming* the twenty-seven books of the New Testament, which is not available until the fourth century. But just because there is no surviving list of a twenty-seven-book canon before the fourth century does not prove one did not exist. It demonstrates that we have no specific record—period. If that method were used in murder trials, only the accused who had *eyewitnesses* testifying against them would be convicted. Circumstantial evidence, no matter how strong, would never convict an accused murderer.

Ridderbos contends, "A historical judgment cannot be final and the sole ground for the acceptance of the New Testament as canonical by the church. To do so would mean that the church would base its faith on the results of a historical investigation" (Ridderbos, p. 36).

The Liberal Theory In his book, *The Canon of the Old Testament* (1892), H. E. Ryle popularized the theory that the Old Testament canon took shape in three stages (Bruce, *The Canon of Scripture*, hereafter CS, p. 36). Calling it the liberal theory, Archer explains that according to this notion, Moses did not write the Torah. It developed over many years. The earliest written document was written about 850 BC. Other portions were added between 750 and

650 BC. At the time of Josiah's reform, Deuteronomy became the first part of the Pentateuch to achieve canonicity (2 Kings 23). During the Babylonian Exile (587-539 BC), the priestly sections were written by the Levitical authors under the inspiration of Ezekiel, and their activity continued down to the time of Ezra. Nehemiah 8:1-8 records the first public reading of the entire Torah as "the book of the Law of Moses." Some parts of it had been newly finished. The people were convinced that these five books were the products of Moses' pen and contained the authoritative Word of God. Thus, the canonization of the Torah was in 444 BC. The books of the prophets were gradually assembled into an authoritative list between 300 and 200 BC. The Prophets achieved canonical status under unknown circumstances at a place unknown at a time unknown, but approximately 200 BC. Most of the third division was not even written until after the collection of the Prophets began. The tentative canonization of the third division was between 150 and 100 BC (Archer, pp. 70-71).

Bruce remarks that this account is "completely hypothetical: there is no evidence for it, either in the Old Testament itself or elsewhere" (Bruce, CS, p. 36). Archer points out that it is based on "rationalistic, anti-supernaturalistic presuppositions" and that it rejects "all biblical data which testify to direct revelation from God" (Archer, p. 70). Archer insists, "The Pentateuch affirms with great frequency, 'Jehovah said unto Moses, 'Speak unto the children of Israel and say unto them.' But scholars who do not believe that God could ever speak personally and intelligibly to Moses (or any other man) must reject all such Biblical statements as legendary" (Archer, p. 70).

Harrison says, "For liberal scholars, the formation of the Scriptural corpus was nothing more than a type of human activity in which certain books were regarded as canonical because they had demonstrated their pragmatic value in religious usage. However, such a theory has to face the fact that although works such as Ecclesiasticus and 1 Maccabees had undoubted value for Judaism, they failed to secure a place in the canon of Scripture" (R. K. Harrison, pp. 283-284).

Summary: A discussion of canonicity involves understanding several terms and theories of canonicity.

Campenhausen concludes, "It is possible, nevertheless, given the requisite caution, to reconstruct the main lines of the formation of the Canon. The man who wants to know too much loses the thread and, in the end, learns nothing; the man who turns his attention to what is actually there perceives, to his astonishment, that the links are by no means so obscure as had at first appeared. The right course is not to concentrate simply on isolated individual texts but—more in the manner of the historian than the literary critic—to observe those lines that link up and finally form a discernible pattern" (Campenhausen, p. ix).

So, what can be said about the formation of the Bible? What data does exist? What can be gleaned from the Bible itself? What information is there from extra-biblical sources? Are there discernible patterns?

Chapter 2

THE FORMATION OF THE OLD TESTAMENT

There is no record inside or outside the Bible concerning the formation of the Hebrew Bible (the Protestant Old Testament). Harrison says, "While the Bible legitimately ought to be allowed to define and describe canonicity, it has, in point of fact, almost nothing to say about the manner in which holy writings were assembled or the personages who exercised an influence over the corpus during the diverse stages of its growth. Historical investigation is no more fruitful in uncovering significant information about the activities of synods or other authoritative bodies with regard to the formation of the Old Testament canon than any other form of study" (R. K. Harrison, p. 262). Unger states, "Precisely when or how the entire group of Old Testament books was set apart and definitely recognized as the Word of God is veiled in obscurity" (Unger, p. 73).

Nevertheless, based on what the Bible says, it is possible to put together a likely scenario of how the Old Testament was formed.

The Writings of Moses

The formation of the Bible began with the writings of Moses.

God Spoke God spoke to Moses. The words "God said" occur ten times in the first chapter of Genesis. The same thing is recorded in the other four books Moses wrote (Ex. 6:2; 20:1; Lev. 1:1; Num. 1:1; Deut. 2:2; etc.).

Moses Wrote At God's direction, Moses wrote the words of God. "So Moses came and told the people all the words of the LORD and all the judgments. And all the people answered with one voice and said, 'All the words which the LORD has said we will do.' And Moses wrote all the words of the LORD. And he rose early in the morning and built an altar at the foot of the mountain, and twelve pillars according to the twelve tribes of Israel" (Ex. 24:3-4; see also Ex. 17:14, 34:27; Deut. 17:18, 27:3). Moses wrote the *words* (plural) of the Lord. As an example, notice how often in the book of Numbers, Moses says he is writing what God said (Num. 1:1; 2:1; 3:5; 4:1; 5:1; 5:5; 6:1; 7:4; 8:1; 9:1; 10:1; 11:16; 12:5-6; 13:1; 14:11; 14:20; 15:1; 16:20; 17:1; 18:1; 19:1; 20:7; 21:8; 22:9; etc.).

The People Took Note God saw to it that people took note that what Moses wrote was the words of God (Josh. 1:7-8). God worked so that His words to Moses were preserved, recognized as the Word of God, and used as the Word of God.

The Word of God written by Moses was preserved. "So it was, when Moses had completed writing the words of this law in a book when they were finished, that Moses commanded the Levites, who bore the ark of the covenant of the Lord, saying, 'Take this Book of the Law, and put it beside the ark of the covenant of the Lord your God, that it may be there as a witness against you'" (Deut. 31:24-26; 31:9-11). Moses wrote the Word of God in a *book*, which was placed beside the Ark of the Covenant. Thus, the Word of God given to Moses was preserved.

The Word of God, written by Moses, was recognized as the Word of God. Moses said, "And it shall be, on the day when you cross over the Jordan to the land which the LORD your God is giving you, that you shall set up for yourselves large stones, and whitewash them with lime. You shall write on them all the words of this law, when you have crossed over, that you may enter the land which the LORD your God is giving you, 'a land flowing with milk and honey,' just as the LORD God of your fathers promised you. Therefore it shall be when you have crossed over the Jordan, *that* on Mount Ebal you shall set up these stones, which I command you today, and you shall whitewash them with lime" (Deut. 27:2-4). When the children of Israel arrived in the land, they did as Moses instructed so that the people of God acknowledged the Word of God (Josh. 8:30-35).

The Word of God, written by Moses, was used as the Word of God. What Moses wrote was not preserved in a museum to satisfy people's curiosity. It was preserved for use. When Moses died, God told his successor, Joshua, to hear and heed what Moses wrote: "Only be strong and very courageous, that you may observe to do according to all the law which Moses My servant commanded you; do not turn from it to the right hand or to the left, that you may prosper wherever you go. This Book of the Law shall not depart from your mouth, but you shall meditate in it day and night, that you may observe to do according to all that is written in it. For then you will make your way prosperous, and then you will have good success" (Josh. 1:7-8). God spoke of the "book" of the Law. The five books of Moses were considered one book of "the Law." The *book* of the Law was to be thought about, talked about, and obeyed. The written Word of God was to be used.

As Moses had instructed, Joshua made the Word of God available to the people. "Now Joshua built an altar to the LORD God of Israel in Mount Ebal, as Moses the servant of the LORD had commanded the children of Israel, as it is written in the Book of the Law of Moses: 'an altar of whole stones over which no man has wielded an iron *tool.*' And they offered burnt offerings to the LORD on it and sacrificed peace offerings. And there, in the presence of the children of Israel, he wrote on the stones a copy of the law of Moses, which he had written. Then all Israel, with their elders and officers and judges, stood on either side of the ark before the priests, the Levites, who bore the ark of the covenant of the LORD, the stranger as well as he who was born among them. Half of them *were* in front of Mount Gerizim and half of them in front of Mount Ebal, as Moses, the servant of the LORD had commanded before, that they should bless the people of Israel. And afterward he read all the words of the law, the blessings and the cursings, according to all that is written in the Book of the Law. There was not a word of all that Moses had commanded which Joshua did not read before all the assembly of Israel, with the women, the little ones, and the strangers who were living among them" (Josh. 8:30-35).

There is a question as to how much of the Law was written. Some suggest that Joshua wrote the Ten Commandments (Woudstra says that it is also possible that Joshua wrote the blessings and curses). Others believe that what he wrote was the blessings and cursings of Deuteronomy 27 and 28 (Bush). The Jews believed that what was written was the 613 commandments of the Pentateuch (see Woudstra). Still others have concluded that it was the whole book of Deuteronomy.

It is possible that all five books of Moses were written in stone. Archeologists have discovered inscribed pillars from six to eight feet in height in the Middle East. Some of these inscriptions were three times the length of the book of Deuteronomy (Campbell). Later in history, daily "newspapers" were chiseled in stone six feet high and three feet wide. Tourists today can see examples of such stone newspapers in the ruins of ancient Ephesus.

Note the process: God spoke. Moses wrote what God said. The written Word of God was preserved (Deut. 31:24-26), was to be recognized as the Word of God (Deut. 27:2-4), and was to be used as the Word of God (Deut. 17:18-20). The people noted that what was written was the Word of God (Josh. 1:7-8; 8:30-35).

From the very beginning of the written Word of God and throughout the history of Israel, the Law was recognized and used as the Word of God. The Law of Moses was to be written in a *book* for the king (Deut. 17:18-20). Joshua was to meditate on "the *book* of the Law," talk about it, and obey it (Jos. 1:7-8). The

Law was put on public display (Josh. 8:30-35; see also *"book* of the Law of Moses" in Josh. 23:6). David charged Solomon to obey the commandment of the Lord "as it is written in the Law of Moses" (1 Kings 2:1-3). Amaziah "executed his servants who had murdered his father the king, but the children of the murderers he did not execute, according to what is written in the *Book* of the Law of Moses, in which the LORD commanded, saying, 'Fathers shall not be put to death for their children, nor shall children be put to death for their fathers; but a person shall be put to death for his own sin'" (2 Kings 14:5-6; 21:8). In the days of Josiah the *"book* of the Law" was recognized as the Word of God (2 Kings 22:8-23:1-2). After the rebuilding of the Temple, "They assigned the priests to their divisions and the Levites to their divisions, over the service of God in Jerusalem, as it is written in the *Book* of Moses" (Ezra 6:18). After the return from exile, Ezra read "the *book* of the Law" publicly (Neh. 8:1-5). Nehemiah read "from the *Book* of Moses in the hearing of the people (Neh. 13:1). Malachi wrote, "Remember the Law of Moses, My servant, Which I commanded him in Horeb for all Israel, *With the* statutes and judgments" (Mal. 4:4). All were to meditate in the Law of the Lord (Ps. 1:2). From the time of Moses to the end of the history of Israel in the Old Testament, the Law was called a "book" (Deut. 17:18-20; Jos. 1:7-8; Neh. 8:1-5).

Thus, the book of Moses established a "canon," a *collection* of books recognized as the Word of God (Josh. 1:7-8; 8:30-35). With his writings, the "Bible" was born. The writing of Moses furnished a foundation for all subsequent writings and supplied the concept of canonicity (see R. K. Harrison, p. 265).

Other Writings

God Spoke Many others in ancient Israel claimed God spoke to them (Isa. 1:1-2; Jer. 1:1-4; Ezek. 1:1-3; 32:1-3; Hosea 1:1; Joel 1:1; Amos 1:1-3; Obad. 1; Jonah 1:1; Micah 1:1; Nahum 1:1, 12; Hab. 1:1; 2:1-2; Zeph. 1:1; Haggai 1:1; Zech. 1:1; 1:4-6; Mal. 1:1). The Old Testament explicitly says God spoke through prophets: "Yes, they made their hearts like flint, refusing to hear the law and the words which the LORD of hosts had sent by His Spirit through the former prophets. Thus great wrath came from the LORD of hosts" (Zech. 7:12). Many parts of the Old Testament claim to be the Word of God. It is said that such expressions as "the Lord said," "the Lord spoke," and "the Word of the Lord came" are found 3,808 times in the Old Testament. The New Testament says, "For prophecy never came by the will of man, but holy men of God spoke *as they were* moved by the Holy Spirit" (2 Pet. 1:21).

Men Wrote Those to whom God spoke ("moved") wrote the Word of God given to them (see the long list of references in the previous paragraph!). First Samuel says Samuel "wrote *it* in a book and laid *it* up before the LORD" (1 Sam. 10:25). Keil and Delitzsch say, "It was no doubt placed in the tabernacle, where the Law of Moses was also deposited, by the side of the fundamental law of the divine state in Israel." As Gill points out, in the Tabernacle, it would be accessible, at least by a priest, safe and preserved for future use.

People Took Note People took note that what these authors wrote was the written Word of God, and they used it as the Word of God (Zech. 7:12). In other words, the Old Testament began with the writings of Moses, and as other inspired writings were produced, God saw to it that they were recognized as His Word.

For example, Isaiah quotes Mich (*cf.* Micah 4:1-3 with Isaiah 2:2-4). Keil says Micah wrote first and Delitzsch proves that in his commentary on Isaiah (Micah wrote between 735 and 710 BC; Isaiah wrote in 680 BC).

The elders of Jeremiah's day quote Micah. Jeremiah records, "Then certain of the elders of the land rose up and spoke to all the assembly of the people, saying: 'Micah of Moresheth prophesied in the days of Hezekiah king of Judah, and spoke to all the people of Judah, saying, 'Thus says the LORD of hosts: 'Zion shall be plowed *like* a field, Jerusalem shall become heaps of ruins, And the mountain of the temple like the bare hills of the forest'" (Jer. 26:17-18). In Jeremiah 26:18, the elders quote Micah 3:12 as an inspired utterance of the Lord. Micah prophesied in the days of Hezekiah, who reigned from 715-686 BC. These elders lived in the days of Jehoiakim (Jer. 26:1), who reigned from 609-598 AD! In other words, they are quoting Micah, who preached about a hundred years before, which indicates that they must be quoting what Micah wrote. Laetsch says, "One hundred years after Micah had spoken, these elders were able to quote the text that has come down to us verbatim. A remarkable testimony for the general accuracy of the copies current among the people and handed down through the centuries!" (Laetsch, p. 221). Thompson says,

"The quotation of Mic. 3:12 shows that the oracles of the prophets were preserved and were well known" (Thompson, p. 527). The elders acknowledged that what Micah had written one hundred years before was the Word of God.

Jeremiah wrote what he was commanded to write and *Daniel* recognized what *Jeremiah* wrote as the Word of God. Jeremiah wrote, "Now it came to pass in the fourth year of Jehoiakim the son of Josiah, king of Judah, that this word came to Jeremiah from the LORD, saying: 'Take a scroll of a book and write on it all the words that I have spoken to you against Israel, against Judah, and against all the nations, from the day I spoke to you, from the days of Josiah even to this day'" (Jer. 36:1-2). One of the things Jeremiah prophesied was that the captivity would last seventy years (Jer. 25:8-12; 29:10; Dan. 9:2). The seventy years began when Nebuchadnezzar conquered Jerusalem (Jer. 25:8-12), which began in 605 BC. Seventy years later, Daniel said, "In the first year of his reign I, Daniel, understood by the books the number of the years specified by the word of the Lord, given through Jeremiah the prophet, that He would accomplish seventy years in the desolations of Jerusalem" (Dan. 9:2). Daniel was reading "the books," when he found "the word of the LORD through Jeremiah the prophet." Some say that the article ("the") "does not denote a collection of known sacred writings in which the writings of Jeremiah were included" (Keil). Others claim that the article likely indicates a "collection, recognized as sacred" (Wood). Baldwin says, it indicates "prophetic books were considered canonical at the time of writing." Seventy years after Jeremiah wrote, Daniel acknowledged that what he wrote was the Word of God.

Unger argues that passages such as Nehemiah 9:26-31, Zechariah 1:4, 7:7, 7:12 and Malachi 3:7 "demonstrate that the words of the prophets were believed to have had the same divine sanction as the Mosaic Law" because "a similar divine penalty was meted out upon the transgression of the one as of the other" (Unger, p. 61). Ryrie says, "The prophets claimed to be speaking the Word of God, and their prophecies were recognized as authoritative. Notice these references: Joshua 6:26 compared with 1 Kings 16:34; Joshua 24:29-33 compared with Judges 2:8-9; 2 Chronicles 36:22-23 compared with Ezra 1: 1-4; Daniel 9:2 compared with Jeremiah 25:11-12" (Ryrie, p. 106).

Note the process: God spoke. Men wrote what God said. People took note that what they wrote was the Word of God.

Summary: The formation of the Bible began with the writings of Moses, and as God inspired other books, He saw to it that they were recognized, preserved, and used as His Word.

The Old Testament is not just a collection of all the books written in ancient Israel. Other books were written that did not become part of the Old Testament. For example, 1 Chronicles says, "Now the acts of King David, first and last, indeed they *are* written in the book of Samuel, the seer, in the book of Nathan the prophet, and in the book of Gad, the seer" (1 Chron. 29:29; see Unger p. 52 for a list of others). These were books written by *prophets*. What they wrote might have been true, but God did not inspire it to be part of His Word.

Moreover, the people were warned not to add anything to what God said. "You shall not add to the word which I command you, nor take from it, that you may keep the commandments of the LORD your God which I command you" (Deut. 4:2). "Whatever I command you, be careful to observe it; you shall not add to it nor take away from it" (Deut 12:32). "Every word of God *is* pure; He *is* a shield to those who put their trust in Him. Do not add to His words, Lest He rebuke you, and you be found a liar" (Prov. 30:5-6). Such statements "reminded the Jews of the sacredness of that inspired text" (McDonald, p. 75).

So, if God inspired some books and not others and if He warned His people not to add to His Word, it is reasonable to assume that He providentially worked to see to it that His books were collected. Many scholars have reached the same conclusions.

Young says, "In His good providence, God brought it about that His people should recognize and receive His Word. How He planted this conviction in their hearts with respect to the identity of His Word, we may not be able fully to understand or explain" (Young, p. 168).

Unger observes, "It would be highly unreasonable to suppose that God, who deigned to reveal Himself to man and so overshadowed and worked upon man that he might receive and record the revelation inerrantly, would not continue to exert His power providentially in preserving the precious documents from destruction and in guiding in their eventual collection and arrangement as a complete and authoritative whole" (Unger, pp. 46-47).

Archer says, "The Biblical authors indicate very clearly, whenever the matter comes up, that the various books of the Bible were canonical from the moment of their inception, by virtue of the divine authority ('Thus saith the Lord') behind them, and the books received immediate recognition and acceptance by the faithful as soon as they were made aware of the writings" (Archer, p. 71). Archer argues that it was simply a matter of recognition of the quality inherent in the inspired books. He illustrates: "When a child recognizes his own parents from a multitude of other adults, he does not impart any new quality of parenthood by such an act; he simply recognizes a relationship which already exists. So also with a list of authoritative books drawn up by ecclesiastical synods or councils. They did not impart canonicity to a single page of Scripture; they simply acknowledged the divine inspiration of religious documents which were inherently canonical from the time they were first composed and formally rejected other books for which canonicity had been falsely claimed" (Archer, pp. 69-70).

Harrison says, "The Spirit of God that inspired these compositions also worked in the hearts and minds of the chosen people to testify to them that the writings were in fact the divine Word. It was this witness, in conjunction with the conscious human response, that was evidently the ultimate determining agent in the formulation of the canon. Had the question of canonicity merely rested upon purely academic decisions without an acknowledged concept of inspiration, it is impossible to see how the Jews could ever have come to accept the Old Testament books as being of divine authority" (R. K. Harrison, p. 284).

There are indications of a Jewish canon outside the Old Testament. The book of Sirach, also known as Ecclesiasticus (ca. 190 BC), speaks of the "Law of the Most High" (Sirach 39:1). It also says, "It was Ezekiel who saw the glorious vision, which was showed him upon the chariot of the cherubim. For he made mention of the enemies under the figure of the rain, and directed them that went right. And of the twelve prophets let the memorial be blessed, and let their bones flourish again out of their place: for they comforted Jacob, and delivered them by assured hope" (Sirach 49:8-10).

McDonald says, "This passage is in the heart of Sirach's celebrated 'history of famous men,' which illustrates significant familiarity with the Law and Prophets, which begins in Sir. 44:1 with the words, 'Let us now sing the praises of famous men, our ancestors in their generations.' Sirach shows an awareness of the books of Joshua (46:1-6), Samuel (46:13-47:11), and Kings (47:12-49:3) as well as several other well-known names in the OT writings: Isaiah (48:20-25), Jeremiah (49:6-7), Ezekiel (49:8), and the Twelve Prophets (49:10). His reference to the 'Twelve Prophets' suggests that by the time that Sirach wrote (180 B.C.E), all of the Minor Prophets were collected in one scroll. The entire passage, Sir. 44:1-49:10 suggests that the heroes described in these prophetic writings were familiar to the Jews, that they probably were widely acknowledged in a scriptural or authoritative manner, and that their authors were viewed as spokespersons for God. Sirach does not introduce these famous persons (except for Elijah

[48:10]) but assumes widespread knowledge of them. His purpose was not to celebrate their writings but to celebrate their lives. Whether their writings were identified as Scripture is not obvious, but Sirach's knowledge of them is at least suggestive of their authoritative role in the Judaism of his day" (McDonald, pp. 82-83).

The Prologue to Sirach (ca. 130 BC) was written by the grandson of Sirach, who translated his grandfather's work into Greek and added a prologue. The Prologue says, "Many great teachings have been given to us through the Law and the prophets and the others that followed them, and for these, we should praise Israel for instruction and wisdom. Now, those who read the scriptures must not only themselves understand them but must also, as lovers of learning, be able through the spoken and written word to help the outsiders. So my grandfather Jesus, who had devoted himself, especially to the reading of the Law and the prophets and the other books of our ancestors, and had acquired considerable proficiency in them, was himself also led to write something pertaining to instruction and wisdom so that by becoming familiar also with his book those who love learning might make even greater progress in living according to the law." This is the oldest known reference to a threefold division of the Old Testament, consisting of the Law, Prophets, and other books (Archer, pp. 62-63; R. K. Harrison, p. 270). The threefold division indicates a canon.

Second Maccabees (ca. 124 BC) says, "The same things are reported in the records and in the memoirs of Nehemiah, and also that he founded a library and collected the books about the kings and prophets, and the writings of David, and letters of kings about votive offerings. In the same way, Judas [Maccabeus] also collected all the books that had been lost on account of the war that had come upon us, and they are in our possession. So if you have need of them, send people to get them for you" (2 Macc. 2:13-15). McDonald explains, "This tradition claims that Nehemiah collected books for a library comprising the books of the 'kings' (1-2 Samuel and 1-2 Kings?), the 'prophets,' and the 'writings of David' (the psalms?)" (McDonald, p. 85). Surely, his collection included the Law (Neh. 8:1-5, 13:1).

The Dead Sea Scrolls may be an indication of an Old Testament canon. Ryrie points out that "about 175 of the 500 Dead Sea scrolls are biblical. There are several copies of many of the books of the Old Testament, and all the Old Testament books are represented among the scrolls, except Esther. The existence of biblical books among the scrolls does not in itself prove their canonicity since some of the non-canonical books are also present. However, many of the Dead Sea Scrolls are commentaries, and so far, all of those commentaries deal only with canonical books. That seems to show that a distinction between canonical and non-canonical books was recognized. Also, twenty of the thirty-nine books of the Old Testament are quoted or referred to as Scripture. In summary, the scrolls give positive evidence for the canonicity of all but Chronicles, Esther, and the Song of Solomon" (Ryrie, pp. 106-07). Also, a quotation from one of the scrolls indicates a threefold division (see McDonald, pp. 90-93; his object is that the individual books are not mentioned.).

Around A.D. 40, Philo refers to the same threefold division (*Contemplative Life*, II, 475) and so does Josephus (A.D. 37-100, *Against Apion*, 1:8, quoted below).

Chapter 3

THE FINAL FORMATION OF THE OLD TESTAMENT

There is no record of the *final* formation of the Old Testament into a single volume. Based on what the Old Testament says, it is safe to assume that when God stopped speaking, the formation of the canon stopped. There are indications this did happen.

The Promise in Malachi

Malachi concludes his book with a promise of a prophet who will come just before the Day of the Lord (Mal. 4:5). Ryrie says, "In Malachi 4:5, there is an indication that the prophetic witness would end with Malachi and not begin again until the coming of an Elijah-type prophet in the person of John the Baptist (Matt. 17: 11-12)" (Ryrie, p. 106).

A Comment in 1 Maccabees

The Apocryphal book of 1 Maccabees (ca. 100 BC) says, "There was great distress in Israel, such as has not been since the timethe prophets ceased to appear among them" (1 Maccabees 9:27). In other words, about 100 BC it was recognized that God had not sent a prophet to Israel in some time, which implies that no more Scripture had been written.

A Statement in Josephus

Josephus (AD 37-95) writes, "For we have not an innumerable multitude of books among us, disagreeing from and contradicting one another [as the Greeks have], but only twenty-two books, which contain the records of all the past times; which are justly believed to be divine; and of them five belong to Moses, which contain his laws and the traditions of the origin of mankind till his death. This interval of time was a little short of three thousand years, but as to the time from the death of Moses till the reign of Artaxerxes, king of Persia, who reigned after Xerxes, the prophets, who were after Moses, wrote down what was done in their times in thirteen books. The remaining four books contain hymns to God and precepts for the conduct of human life. It is true, our history hath been written since Artaxerxes very particularly, but hath not been esteemed of the like authority with the former by our forefathers, because there hath not been an exact succession of prophets since that time; and how firmly we have given credit to those books of our own nation, is evident by what we do; for during so many ages as have already passed, no one has been so bold as either to add anything to them, to take anything from them, or to make any change in them; but it becomes natural to all Jews, immediately and from their very birth, to esteem those books to contain divine doctrines, and to persist in them, and, if occasion be, willingly to die for them. For it is no new thing for our captives, many of them in number, and frequently in time, to be seen to endure racks and deaths of all kinds upon the theatres, that they may not be obliged to say one word against our laws and the records that contain them; whereas there are none at all among the Greeks who would undergo the least harm on that account, no, nor in case all the writings that are among them were to be destroyed; for they take them to be such discourses as are famed agreeably to the inclinations of those that write them; and they have justly the same opinion of the ancient writers, since they see some of the present generation bold enough to write about such affairs, wherein they were not present, nor had concern enough to inform themselves about them from those that knew them: examples of which may be had in this late war of ours, where some persons have written histories, and published them, without having been in the places concerned, or having been near them when the actions were done; but these men put a few things together by hearsay, and insolently abuse the world, and call these writings by the name of Histories" (Josephus, *Against Apion*, 1:8).

The Content of the Jewish Canon According to Josephus, a first-century Jew, the Jews had twenty-two books they believed to be divine. He says those twenty-two books consisted of the five books of Moses, thirteen from the prophets, and four containing "hymns to God, and precepts for the conduct of human life." The question is, "How does the twenty-two-book canon of Josephus compare to the Hebrew Bible and the Protestant Old Testament?"

The Formation of The Bible

The Hebrew Bible contains twenty-four books, beginning with Genesis and ending with 2 Chronicles (see the traditional Masoretic text). Does that mean that the Hebrew Bible contains two more books than the list of Josephus? No. It has been suggested that Josephus arrived at twenty-two books by combining Ruth with Judges and Lamentations with Jeremiah (Bruce, CS, p. 33). Origen pointed out there are twenty-two letters in the Hebrew alphabet (Unger, p. 55).

The Protestant Old Testament has thirty-nine books. Does that mean it has more books than Josephus? No. Following the Septuagint, the Greek translation of the Hebrew Bible (250-160 BC), the Protestant Bible divides the books of Samuel, Kings, Chronicles, and Ezra-Nehemiah into two books each (making eight instead of four). It divides the Twelve Minor Prophets into individual books (making twelve instead of one). Thus, fifteen additional books (4+11=15) appear to be added, but there is no further material, only a different division (Unger, p. 54). The arrangement is also different. The Hebrew Bible begins with Genesis and closes with 2 Chronicles. The Protestant Old Testament begins with Genesis and ends with Malachi, but the content is exactly the same as the Hebrew Bible. Thus, the twenty-four-book division of the Hebrew Bible is identical to the thirty-nine-book division of the Protestant Old Testament. The only difference is the division and the order (Unger, p. 54).

In other words, the twenty-two book division of Josephus is identical to the twenty-four book division of the Masoretic text, which is the same as the thirty-nine book division of the Protestant

Old Testament. *The Divisions of the Jewish Canon* Josephus speaks of a threefold division consisting of the Law, the Prophets, and Hymns. *The Final Formation of the Jewish Canon* According to Josephus, anything written after Artaxerxes has not been esteemed with the same authority as the former divine works because there has not been an "exact succession of prophets since that time." He clearly says, "No one has been so bold as either to add anything to them, to take anything from them, or to make any change in them; but it becomes natural to all Jews, immediately and from their very birth to esteem, those books to contain divine doctrines, and to persist in them, and, if occasion be, willingly to die for them." He adds that this is unlike anything non-Jews would do.

Later, a rabbinic tradition claimed, "When the latter prophets died, that is, Haggai, Zechariah and Malachi, then the Holy Spirit became to an end in Israel" (*Sotah* 13:2, Neusner, *Tosefta*, 885, cited by McDonald, p. 419).

Bruce observes that Josephus does not mean the gift of prophecy died out because he mentions its exercise among the Essenes (Josephus, *Antiquities*, 13:311, 15.373-379), by John Hycanus (134-104 BC; Josephus, 13:300), and he even claims to have had the gift himself (Josephus, *Jewish Wars* 3:351-354; Bruce, CS, p. 33). As Archer explains, Josephus says, "No more canonical writings have been composed since the reign of Artaxerxes, son of Xerxes (464-424 B.C.), i.e., since the time of Malachi." Furthermore, "No additional material was ever included in the canonical twenty-two books during the centuries between (i.e., from 424 B. C. to A.D. 90)" (Archer, p. 64).

In other words, based on what Josephus wrote, the content of the Hebrew Bible, the threefold division of the Hebrew Bible, and his statement about the cessation of prophets indicate there was a final formation of the Old Testament canon since Artaxerxes, whose dates are 465-425 BC (Unger, p. 71).

Summary: There is no record of a *final* formation of the Old Testament into a single volume, but the promise of Malachi implies there would be no more prophets until the arrival of a prophet before the Day of the Lord, and Josephus indicates that there were no more prophets after the time of Artaxerxes. Thus, it is safe to assume that when God stopped speaking, the formation of the Old Testament canon stopped.

Chapter 4

FORMAL RECOGNITION OF THE OLD TESTAMENT

There is no record of a "formal recognition" of the Old Testament. No surviving document, either from Judaism or Christianity, gives definite answers to the questions of the formal recognition of the Old Testament.

Theories

The Great Synagogue There is a tradition that attributes the formation of the canon to Ezra and the men of The Great Synagogue, but "the history of that body is itself wrapped in obscurity" (Unger, p. 73; R. K. Harrison, p. 275).

Earlier it was pointed out that 2 Maccabees (ca. 124 BC) said, "The same things are reported in the records and in the memoirs of Nehemiah, and also that he founded a library and collected the books about the kings and prophets, and the writings of David, and letters of kings about votive offerings" (2 Macc. 2:13) and that McDonald explains, "This tradition claims that Nehemiah collected books for a library comprising the books of the 'kings' (1-2 Samuel and 1-2 Kings?), the 'prophets,' and the 'writings of David' (the psalms?)" (McDonald, p. 85). Surely, he included the Law (Neh. 8:1-5, 13:1).

Also, Josephus said there were no prophets after the time of Artaxerxes, whose dates are 465-425 BC (see the previous chapter).

Baker suggests, "While much of the tradition about the Great Synagogue is no doubt fanciful and contrary to fact, it is altogether reasonable that the last five writers of the Old Testament who were more or less contemporaneous, Ezra, Nehemiah, Haggai, Zechariah, and Malachi, were responsible for not only restoring the political and religious life of Israel after the Captivity but also for collecting the sacred writings along with the books they were led to write. There were no inspired writers after their time who would have been in a position to do so important work and thus, it seems most reasonable to believe that there is some basic truth associated with the tradition that the Canon was formed under the leadership of Ezra, the founder of the guild of the Scribes" (Baker, p. 82).

Ezra (ca. 440 BC), Malachi (ca. 430 BC), and Nehemiah (ca. 425 BC) were the last to write and it is reasonable to assume that they collected all the inspired books.

The Time of the Maccabees Beckwith proposes that the Jewish canon probably reached its final form in the time of Judas Maccabaeus, which was about 164 BC (Hill, p. 442).

The Council of Jamnia Many scholars have theorized that the final ratification of the Hebrew Bible was in A.D. 90 at the council of Jamnia, a small town about thirty miles from Jerusalem near Jaffa. After the destruction of Jerusalem in A.D. 70, Jewish religious leaders met at Jamnia to clarify how Judaism could survive without the Temple and the sacrifices.

The problem with the theory is that they ratified the Hebrew Bible, but there is no evidence that the rabbis established a Hebrew canon at that meeting. They raised questions about the presence of Esther, Proverbs, Ecclesiastes, the Song of Songs, and Ezekiel in the canon, but there was no thought of removing these books from the canon. The issue was not so much accepting writings into the canon but their right to remain there (R. K. Harrison, pp. 277-279; for a summary of the discussion of the canon at Jamnia, see Bruce, CS, pp. 34-36). McDonald says this view is now largely abandoned (McDonald, pp. 173-175).

An Observation Formal recognition did not determine canonicity; inspiration did. Unger observes, "Canonization of books is not to be confounded with their collection. Books were not made canonical because of their collection. They were collected because they were canonical, i.e., possessed of divine authority by virtue of their inspired character. Consequently, the ancient Jews had a canon of Scripture long before their holy writings were *formally arranged in the three-fold division* and as a unified whole. It is at this point the critical theory transgresses. It makes canonicity dependent upon formal collection and arrangement and fails to see the clear distinction that must be observed between the two concepts. Canonicity is quite independent of formal collection and arrangement. Formal collection and arrangement are *not*, however, independent of canonicity" (Unger, p. 76).

Ryrie agrees, "The books were canonical the moment they were written. It was not necessary to wait until various councils could examine the books to determine if they were acceptable or not. Their canonicity was inherent within them since they came from God. People and councils only recognized and acknowledged what is true because of the intrinsic inspiration of the books as they were written. No Bible book became canonical by the action of some church council" (Ryrie, p. 105).

Conclusion Unger says, "The simplest and best view, which does not run counter to the internal evidence and claims of the Hebrew Scriptures themselves, is that as these books were written by a prophet of God, usually with an established reputation (Jeremiah 36), beginning with Moses, they were at the time, recognized as inspired of God and deposited in the Tabernacle or Temple, along with the accumulating store of Holy Oracles. Official Tabernacle or Temple copies were jealously guarded and carefully copied as new scrolls were needed. When many copies were destroyed and scattered in the fall of Jerusalem to the Babylonians, it was Ezra who restored the Scriptures as a complete group to their place in the second Temple. In the post-exilic period, other copies were made from Temple copies for use in widely dispersed synagogues. Since the writings of the prophets, as soon as they were issued, had intrinsic authority as inspired Scripture, 'no formal declaration of their canonicity was needed to give them sanction' (Green). God, who had divinely inspired these writings, we may reasonably believe, moved providentially in behalf of their acceptance by the faithful and godly. However, their inspiration and consequent divine authority were *inherent* and *not* dependent on human reception or lapse of time to give them prestige or until there were no more living prophets or *any other factor*. The canon does not derive its authority from the sanction of Jewish priests and leaders or from the Christian Church. *That authority is in itself.* The collection of the canon is merely the assembling into one volume of those books whose sacred character and claim have already secured general acknowledgment" (Unger, pp. 73-74).

Confirmation

While there is no biblical or historical record of a formal recognition of the Old Testament, there is confirmation that there was a closed canon in the first century.

Names in the New Testament The New Testament uses names for the Old Testament that seem to be referring to "the whole Old Testament" (Thiessen, p. 4), such as "the Scripture" (2 Tim. 3:16; 1 Pet. 2:6) and "the Holy Scriptures" (Rom. 1:2). Jesus calls Psalm 118:22 Scripture (Mt. 21:42). He speaks of "the Scripture" as if there was a collection of books (Mt. 22:29; Lk. 24:32; Jn. 5:39; 10:35). Harrison says, "By the time of Christ, it would seem, the Old Testament existed as a complete collection. The evidence presented by the New Testament writers indicates that the Old Testament as a whole was referred to 'the Scriptures' or 'the Scripture' at that period to designate a familiar and unified group of inspired and authoritative writings" (R. K. Harrison, p. 276). "The very word *Scripture*, as in is used in the New Testament, carries the idea of canonicity, or that which measures up to the divine standard, that which is the authoritative word of God (Baker, p. 76).

Not only is the term "Scripture" used in the New Testament of the whole Old Testament, so is the term "law." Jesus says, "It is written in your law" and quotes Psalm 82:6 (Jn. 10:34). Harrison says the term "law" in John 10:34 refers to the "entire corpus of the Hebrew Scriptures" (R. K. Harrison, p. 265). Paul says, "In the law it is written" (1 Cor. 14:21) and cites Isaiah 28:11-12.

In addition, the expression "the Law and the Prophets" is used of the Old Testament (Mt. 5:17; 7:12; 22:40; Lk. 16:16; 24:27; Acts 13:15; 24:14; 28:23; Rom. 3:21). The Law is, of course, the Law of Moses (Jn. 10:34). The contents of "the Prophets" is never delineated in the Bible, but books in the third division are said to be from the Prophets (Mt. 24:15) and books in the third division are treated as Scripture (Acts 1:16, 2:25-31, 34-36). By using the expression "the Law and the Prophets," Paul certainly seems to be saying that he had the same Scriptures as the Jews (Acts 24:14). In the second century AD, the term "Prophets" is used of the entire Old Testament (McDonald, p. 111, who cites Justin, *1 Apol.* 67). As McDonald says, "Since both Jews and Christians believed that God had inspired all Scripture, all of it was prophetic" (McDonald, p. 111).

Harrison says, "Usually the New Testament writers only mentioned the first two sections (Matt. 5:17; Lk. 16:16), but quite obviously they included the Hagiographa with the Prophets just as the Talmudic teachers did (due perhaps to the lack of a current technical term for the Hagiographa)" (R. K. Harrison, p. 269;

Hagiographa, also called Writings, consist of Psalms, Proverbs, Job, the Song of Solomon, Ruth, Lamentations, Ecclesiastes, Esther, Daniel, Ezra, Nehemiah, and Chronicles).

Ryrie agrees, "This twofold division covers all of the Old Testament" (Ryrie, p. 107). Harrison also points out, "New Testament authors commonly alluded to the Scriptures in terms of two categories—the Law and the Prophets. Support for this position has been provided by the discoveries from Qumran, where in four instances, the Community Rule or Manual of Discipline (lQS, 1:3; VIII:13 ff.) and the Zadokite Fragment (CDC, V:21; VII:15 ff.) referred to the Old Testament writings in precisely the same two categories" (R. K. Harrison, p. 276).

Even McDonald, who does not believe that the Old Testament canon was closed in the first century, says the expression "the Law and the Prophets" appears "to comprise all of the sacred Scriptures" and "sometimes the whole of the sacred writings is referred to simply as 'law'" (McDonald, p. 99)! In his comment on Acts 28:23, Bruce says the expression "the Law of Moses and the prophets" indicates that "his text was the whole volume of what we now called the Old Testament."

Thus, the New Testament uses a wide variety of expressions and terms to refer to the Word of God, including the "Scripture," "Law," "the Law and the prophets," etc. In other words, when the New Testament records an expression like "the Scripture says," it is the same as someone saying today, "The Bible says." Furthermore, The New Testament claims the Old Testament is the Word of God (2 Tim. 14-16; Heb. 1:1; 2 Pet. 1:20, 21).

Statements by Jesus When Jesus said, "Therefore, whatever you want men to do to you, do also to them, for this is the Law and the Prophets" (Mt. 7:12), He obviously meant that the Golden Rule is the sum of the complete Old Testament (Bruce, CS, p. 32).

Jesus mentions the first and last books of the Old Testament. In condemning the religious leaders, He charged them with being guilty of shedding the blood of all the righteous from Abel to Zechariah (Mt. 23:35; Lk. 11:51). The murder of Abel is recorded in Genesis 4, and the murder of Zechariah in 2 Chronicles 24:20-21. Genesis is the first book, and 2 Chronicles is the last book in the Hebrew Bible. So the Lord says, "From the first to the last murder in the Old Testament." Thus, the Hebrew canon was complete by the time of Jesus (Bruce, CS, p. 31). Unger says this can "only have meaning if the final order and arrangement of the Hebrew canon is referred to" (Unger, p. 71).

Luke 24 says, "Beginning at Moses and all the Prophets, He (Jesus) expounded to them in all the Scriptures the things concerning Himself" (Lk. 24:27). The expression "all the prophets" added to the Law of Moses indicates a closed collection of Scriptures.

Later in Luke 24, Jesus said, "All things must be fulfilled which were written in the Law of Moses and *the* Prophets and *the* Psalms concerning Me" (Lk. 24:44). This threefold division of the Old Testament is "used in direct parallel with the phrase 'Moses and the prophets' earlier in the chapter" (Geisler, p. 367). Leiman contends that "Psalms" represents the third division of the Hebrew Bible because it stands first in some Hebrew manuscripts

(S. Z. Leiman, *Canonization of the Hebrew Scripture*, p. 40; see also E. E. Ellis, *The Old Testament in Early Christianity*, p. 9, fn 30). Beckwith says "Psalms" refers to the third part of the Hebrew canon in the Talmudic literature (Beckwith, p. 438). He also says that since Jesus cites the book of Daniel (Dan. 4:26 in Mt. 4:17; Dan. 9:27, 11:31, 12:11 in Mt. 24:15; and Dan. 7:13 in Mk. 14:62), which was a part of the Writings, He intended the whole of the Writings when He mentioned the "Psalms" in Luke 24:44 (Beckwith, pp. 111-112).

Harrison says, "The threefold division of the canon was well established in the early Christian era. The New Testament makes it clear that the canon familiar to Jesus Christ was identical to the one that exists today. None of the Apocrypha or Pseudepigrapha is ever cited by name, much less accorded the status of Scripture, whereas Daniel is specifically quoted as a prophetic composition in Matthew 24:15. The three chief divisions were enumerated in Luke 24:44 as the Law, the Prophets, and the Psalms" (R. K. Harrison, p. 269).

Summary: There is no record of any "formal recognition" of the Old Testament, but it is reasonable to assume that Ezra, Malachi, and Nehemiah, the last to write, collected all the inspired books and the references to the Old Testament in the New Testament confirm that the canon of the Old Testament was closed in the first century.

Chapter 5

THE DEBATE ABOUT THE OLD TESTAMENT

There is a debate over the canon of the Old Testament to this very day. There are books written after the close of the Old Testament that are accepted by some branches of Christianity but not by the Protestants.

The Apocrypha

Explanation: "Apocrypha" refers to a collection of Jewish writings written between 300 BC and A.D. 70. There are fourteen writings or portions of writings in the Apocrypha: Tobit, Judith, Additions to the Book of Esther, Wisdom of Solomon, Sirach (a.k.a. Ecclesiastes), Baruch, Epistle of Jeremiah, Song of the Three Jews, Susanna, Bel and the Dragon, 1 and 2 Maccabees, 1 Esdras, the Prayer of Manasseh, and 2 Esdras.

Of the fourteen, the Roman Catholic Counsel of Trent claimed eleven to be canonical: Tobit, Judith, Additions to the Book of Esther (added to Esther), Wisdom of Solomon, Sirach (a.k.a. Ecclesiastes), Baruch, Song of the Three Jews, Susanna, Bel and the Dragon (added to Daniel), 1 and 2 Maccabees (appearing as separate books). The Roman Catholics generally refer to them as "deuterocanonical." Geisler observes that the Council of Trent accepted 2 Maccabees, a book supporting praying for the dead (2 Maccabees 12:45 [46]), some 29 years after Luther lashed out against praying for the dead (Geisler, p. 365).

Reasons for Rejection The New Testament copiously quotes the Old Testament but does not quote the Apocrypha. Geisler points out, "Jesus himself cited Genesis (Matt. 19:4-5), Exodus (John 6:31), Leviticus (Matt. 8:4), Numbers (John 3:14), Deuteronomy (Matt. 4:4), and I Samuel (Matt. 12:3-4). He also referred to Kings (Luke 4:25) and II Chronicles (Matt. 23:35), as well as Ezra-Nehemiah (John 6:31). Psalms is frequently quoted by Jesus (see Matt. 21:42; 22:44), Proverbs is quoted by Jesus in Luke 14:8-10 (see Provo 25:6-7), and Song of Solomon may be alluded to in John 4:10. Isaiah is often quoted by Christ (see Luke 4:18-19). Likewise, Jesus alludes to Jeremiah's Book of Lamentations (Matt. 27:30) and perhaps to Ezekiel (John 3:10). Jesus specifically quoted Daniel by name (Matt. 24:21). He also quoted passages from the twelve (minor) prophets (Matt. 26:31). Other books, such as Joshua (Heb. 13:5), Ruth (Heb. 11:32), and Jeremiah (Heb. 8:8-12), are quoted by New Testament writers. The teachings of Ecclesiastes are clearly reflected in the New Testament (cf. Gal. 6:7 and Eccles. 11:1 or Heb. 9:27 and Eccles. 3:2)" (Geisler, p. 356). Geisler also observes, "There is no explicit citation of Judges, Chronicles, Esther, or the Song of Solomon, although Hebrews 11:32 refers to events in Judges, II Chronicles 24:20 may be alluded to in Matthew 23:35, Song of Solomon 4:15 may be reflected in John 4:15, and the feast of Purim established in Esther was accepted by the New Testament Jews" (Geisler, pp. 355-356).

The point is that the New Testament contains abundant references to the Old Testament but does not quote the Apocrypha. Some claim that the prophecy of Enoch in Jude 14-15 is from the apocryphal *Book of Enoch*. In the first place, Jude does not say he is quoting the *Book of Enoch*. Indeed, he may not have been. This prophecy of Enoch was no doubt handed down in Jewish tradition. For that matter, he could have gotten it from the Lord himself. After all, Jesus was his half-brother. Furthermore, if Jude quotes the book of Enoch, it does not mean he thought the book of Enoch was inspired. Authors of inspired Scripture quote non-inspired material. It does mean, however, that it is the truth.

There are other reasons for rejecting the Apocrypha. Not only was it never quoted by Jesus or any of the New Testament writers, but it was also never recognized as Scripture by the early Christians. From the beginning, the word "Apocrypha" was used in writings not to be read in public worship but in private, generally by the more mature believers (see McDonald, p. 142). The Roman Catholic Church did not recognize the Apocrypha as Scripture until the Council of Trent in 1546.

Ryrie says, "There are some 250 quotes from Old Testament books in the New Testament. None is from the Apocrypha. All Old Testament books are quoted except Esther, Ecclesiastes, and the Song of Solomon" (Ryrie, p. 107). He also points out that in Luke 11:51, Jesus marks the extent of the Old Testament when He mentions the murders of Abel and Zechariah, but since there were other murders of God's messengers recorded in the Apocrypha after that, the Lord must not have included them in the canon (Ryrie, pp. 107-108).

Harrison says, "There was no controversy at all in connection with the books of the Apocrypha, for everyone agreed that they were non-canonical. The reason appears to have been that the works themselves simply gave no evidence whatever of having been divinely inspired. As Green and others have pointed out, some of these writings contain egregious historical, chronological, and geographical errors, quite apart from justifying falsehood and deception and making salvation dependent upon deeds of merit" (R. K. Harrison, p. 286).

Baker says, "These books were written during the gap between the testaments and while they are valuable for historical reasons, they were never considered canonical by the Jews; they are never quoted in the New Testament; they make no claim to inspiration; they contain historical inaccuracies and they are on a much lower moral and spiritual level than the canonical books" (Baker, p. 85).

Biblical Books

"Certain Jewish teachers of the second century A.D. questioned the canonicity of Song of Solomon, Ecclesiastes, Esther, Ezekiel, and Proverbs, either because they were thought to contain contradictory statements to other parts of Scripture or did not mention the name of God, etc." (Baker, p. 85), but there is evidence from the New Testament that the Old Testament was closed in the first century and all those books are in the Old Testament.

Summary: The Apocryphal books are not part of the collection of inspired books because they were not sanctioned by Jesus or by the writers of the New Testament.

Chapter 6

THE FORMATION OF THE NEW TESTAMENT

As with the Old Testament, based on what the Bible says, it is possible to put together a likely scenario of how the New Testament was formed.

God Spoke

The Promise Jesus promised the apostles that the Holy Spirit would speak to them to reveal to them things to come. He said, "When He, the Spirit of truth, has come, He will guide you into all truth; for He will not speak on His own *authority,* but whatever He hears, He will speak; and He will tell you things to come" (Jn. 16:13; "holy men of God spoke *as they were* moved by the Holy Spirit" in 2 Pet. 1:21). This promise was given to the *apostles*; the Holy Spirit would guide *them* in all truth and declare to *them* things to come.

The Fulfillment Paul claimed that he received the gospel by revelation (Gal. 1:11-12; 1 Cor. 15:3-4), that the Word of the Lord was his source for information about the rapture (1 Thess. 4:15), that Christ spoke through him (2 Cor. 13:3; 1 Cor. 7:10, 7:40; Eph. 3:3; 1 Thess. 4:1) and that he spoke in *words* that the Holy Spirit teaches (1 Cor. 2:13).

Men Wrote

Personal Claim Men wrote the Word of God. For example, Paul says, "If anyone thinks himself to be a prophet or spiritual, let him acknowledge that the things which I write to you are the commandments of the Lord" (1 Cor. 14:37; 2 Thess. 2:15; 2 Thess. 3:14). John says, "For I testify to everyone who hears the words of the prophecy of this book: If anyone adds to these things, God will add to him the plagues that are written in this book; and if anyone takes away from the words of the book of this prophecy, God shall take away his part from the Book of Life, from the holy city, and *from* the things which are written in this book" (Rev. 22:18-19; see Jn. 21:24). McDonald says, "Clearly the author of these words believed that he had the voice of prophecy and was inspired when he wrote" (McDonald, p. 417).

Public Reading The Jews read the Scripture in the Synagogue (Lk. 4:16-21). Believers read the Scripture in church meetings (1 Tim. 4:13). Reading a text in these meetings "implied recognition of its sacredness and authority" (McDonald, p. 144). The New Testament authors commanded that their writings should be read in public. Paul says, "I charge you by the Lord that this epistle be read to all the holy brethren" (1 Thess. 5:27; Col. 4:16). John says, "Blessed *is* he who reads and those who hear the words of this prophecy, and keep those things which are written in it; for the time *is* near" (Rev. 1:3; 2:7, 2:11, 2:17, 2:29; 3:6, 3:13, 3:22).

People Took Note

Discernment One of the spiritual gifts is the "discerning of spirits" (1 Cor. 12:10). John exhorted all believers: "Beloved, do not believe every spirit, but test the spirits, whether they are of God; because many false prophets have gone out into the world" (1 Jn. 4:1). Thus, by the Spirit of God, people took note that what was written was the Word of God. This is illustrated by what Paul told the Thessalonians about his preaching to them: "When you received the word of God which you heard from us, you welcomed *it* not *as* the word of men, but as it is in truth, the word of God, which also effectively works in you who believe" (1 Thess. 2:13).

Recognition There was immediate recognition that what was written was Scripture. Paul called Luke's Gospel Scripture. First Timothy 5:18 says, "For the Scripture says, 'You shall not muzzle an ox while it treads out the grain,' and, 'The laborer is worthy of his wages.'" In this verse, Paul quotes "Scripture" and gives one reference from the Old Testament and another, which is only found in the Gospel of Luke.

Peter called Paul's writings Scripture. Peter says, "That the longsuffering of our Lord is salvation—as also our beloved brother Paul, according to the wisdom given to him, has written to you, as also in all his epistles, speaking in them of these things, in which are some things hard to understand, which those who are untaught and unstable twist to their own destruction, as they do also the rest of the Scriptures" (2 Pet. 3:15, 16). Peter speaks of "all" of Paul's epistles (2 Pet. 3:15), which indicates that Paul's epistles had

had already been collected. Bruce says, "Here Paul's letters seem to form a recognizable collection and to be given the status of scripture since they are associated with 'the other scriptures'" (Bruce, CS, p. 120).

Peter wrote in A.D. 64. Thiessen says, "The process of collecting began almost immediately after the books had been written. Peter already speaks of the Pauline Epistles 'as well known' (Thiessen, p. 7). Ryrie contends that the term 'Scripture' was 'a designation in Judaism for canonical books, so when it is used in the New Testament of other New Testament writings, it designates those writings as canonical'" (Ryrie, p. 108; see also Baker, p. 77).

The use of 2 Peter as first-century evidence for recognizing Paul's epistles as Scripture is dependent on the first-century dating of 2 Peter, which has been rejected by some who say Peter did not write 2 Peter. They reject 2 Peter as genuine because of the differences between the style and vocabulary of 1 and 2 Peter and because there is no early tradition for 2 Peter.

The epistle itself, however, bears abundant testimony to Peter's authorship. It claims to have been written by "Simon Peter" (2 Pet. 1:1). It even claims to be his second letter (2 Pet. 3:1). The author refers to the Lord's prediction about Peter's death (Jn. 21:18-19 and 2 Peter 1:14). He also claims he was an eyewitness of the transfiguration (2 Pet. 1:16-18). As Lumby says, "It is almost inconceivable that a forger, writing to warn against false teachers, writing in the interest of truth, should have thus deliberately assumed a name and experience to which he had no claim" (Thiessen, p. 288).

Concerning the differences between 1 Peter and 2 Peter, "Bigg counts 361 words in I Peter, not in II Peter, while II Peter has 231, not in I Peter. This is indeed a remarkable situation. But the truly remarkable fact is, as Ebright points out, that both epistles have a vocabulary differing much from the rest of the New Testament. 'There are seven times as many rare words in I Peter as in the New Testament taken as a whole and ten times as many in II Peter ... The noticeable difference, therefore, is not between the two Petrine epistles, but between these epistles and the rest of the New Testament' (Biggs, cited by Hiebert, pp. 152-53). As for early evidence, Jude virtually recognized 2 Peter 2 (Jude 5-19). Zahn thinks we have an early attestation of it in the Epistle of Jude and that we really need no other" (Thiessen, p. 287).

Bruce says, "What is important is this: from the early second century onward, Paul's letters circulated not singly, but as a collection." He goes on to say, "The codex into which the letters were copied by their first editor constituted a master copy on which the letters were based" (Bruce, CS, p. 130).

To the church in Philadelphia, Jesus said, "I know your works. See, I have set before you an open door, and no one can shut it; for you have a little strength, have kept My word, and have not denied My name. Indeed, I will make those of the synagogue of Satan, who say they are Jews and are not, but lie; indeed I will make them come and worship before your feet, and to know that I have loved you. Because you have kept My command to persevere, I also will keep you from the hour of trial which shall come upon the whole world, to test those who dwell on the earth" (Rev. 3:8-10).

In A.D. 95, Jesus, through John, could say that they had His word (Rev. 3:8) and they had kept His command (Rev. 3:10). Since they did not hear Him speak, this, at least, implies they had His Word in written form. Did they not have the Gospels by this time?

Nicole suggests a "notable parallel" exists between establishing the Old Testament and New Testament canon. God entrusted the Old Testament Scriptures to the Jews (Rom. 3:2), and "They were providentially guided in the recognition and preservation of the OT. Jesus and the apostles confirmed the rightness of their approach while castigating their attachment to a tradition that was superimposed on the Word of God (Matt 15:1-20; Mark 7:1-23)." Nicole says God entrusted the New Testament to His people in the churches (Nicole, p. 205).

Summary: When God spoke and men wrote the books of the New Testament, people immediately recognized what was written was the Word of God, and there are indications that those books were collected. God saw to it that they were recognized as His Word, preserved, and used as His Word.

The process of collecting began immediately after the New Testament books were written. Harrison points out that Colossians 4:16 refers to the "circulating of an epistle to at least one other church, and the admonition to obtain a second epistle from the other church (Laodicea) that it might be read in the church at Colosse. It is a reasonable inference that neither the writer nor the readers looked upon such documents as having only momentary value. A need for them might well arise elsewhere, warranting their preservation" (Everett Harrison, p. 92). It is hard to imagine that the believers in the church at Colosse did not *copy* the letter from Paul before they sent it (or a copy of it) to Laodicea.

C. F. D. Moule suggested that Luke was one of the first to collect Paul's letters. It would have been in keeping with his historian's temperament (Moule, cited by CS, p. 129). Thiessen's theory is the publication of Acts (A.D. 61) may have "aroused a general interest in all that Paul had written and promoted the collecting and publishing of his writings." He suggests, "Ephesus became a great Christian center during the last half of the first century, and it may well be that these Epistles were first published as a body of Pauline literature in this city." He adds, "The Synoptic Gospels were undoubtedly collected about the same time or only a little later, perhaps also at Ephesus, where the Gospel of John was published and added to the collection late in the first century. It is interesting to note that the Book of Revelation begins with a group of seven letters addressed to seven churches in Asia" (Thiessen, p. 8). Thiessen's theory is interesting because Ephesians, 1 Timothy, 1 John, and Revelation were sent to Ephesus. Warfield asserts that the canon of the New Testament was completed when John finished the book of Revelation (Warfield, p. 455).

It is reasonable to assume that by the end of the first century, there was a collection of Paul's epistles (2 Pet. 3:15) and the four Gospels, if not other New Testament books as well. McDonald, who does not think the canon was closed by the end of the first century, concedes that by the end of the first century, collections of Paul's writings "circulated freely among many churches" (McDonald, p. 321).

As with the Law of Moses, God wanted His Word used. Hence, it was to be read in the assembly. McDonald makes an interesting observation. He points out that the standard book was written on scrolls in the ancient world. This practice continued until the fourth century when the codex began to overtake the scroll, but not much later than A.D.100, the Christian community preferred the codex, the ancient predecessor of the modern book, over the use of the scroll. McDonald says the codex was developed by the Romans and used for nonliterary texts such as business documents, personal notes, memos, and billings. Paul often wrote letters to churches in books (codices) made of papyrus sheets or parchments. McDonald quotes Gamble, who says it was unusual for the early Christians to use the codex for their collection of Scriptures "since it was not recognized in antiquity as a proper book. It was regarded as a mere notebook, and its associations were strictly private and utilitarian." McDonald cites the Roman poet Martial (ca. A.D. 80), who advised his readers to make use of the codex if they wanted to carry his poems on their journeys: "Those that parchment confines in small pages" (Epigram 1.2, LCL). Martial indicated that even the great poets' works, including Homer, Virgil, Cicero, Livy, and Ovid, were transported in this fashion. Gamble also notes that the codex could hold the contents of several scrolls. It provided the convenience of easy access and rapid referencing of material in teaching or debates with opponents.

McDonald concludes, "Because Paul made use of the codex, no doubt for convenience and portability, and because his writings were among the earliest to be acknowledged as Scripture in many churches (2 Pet 3:15-16), it is likely that he is the originator of the use of the codex in early Christianity. When his letters were collected at the end of the first century, it is likely that the use of the codex made it possible to circulate his writings in one volume" (McDonald, pp. 211-212).

Chapter 7

RECOGNITION IN THE EARLY CHURCH

There is no historical record of the *final* formation of the New Testament. Chafer says, "No record exists as to what church first acquired a complete Bible, or the precise date of such an occurrence" (Chafer, vol. 1, p. 92). The writings, however, that have survived from the earliest times of church history indicate that the books of the New Testament were known, and there is evidence that some were recognized as Scripture.

In fact, the writings that were produced *immediately* after the close of the New Testament, that is, from A.D. 95 to A.D. 110, quote or allude to every book of the New Testament, assuming that 2 and 3 John are included with 1 John, which according to Goodspeed early writers, such as Irenaeus, did (see Thiessen, p. 22). See the chart on early references to the New Testament in the appendix.

The Apostolic Fathers

Christian authors who wrote before A.D. 150 are sometimes called the Apostolic Fathers, because of their proximity to the Apostles. Cairns lists people and writings from this period: Clement of

Rome, *The Epistle to Diognetus*, Papias, Polycarp, Ignatius, *The Didache*, and the *Epistle of Barnabas* (Cairns, p. 72). To that list are sometimes added *The Shepherd of Hermas* and *Second Clement*. The definite dating of the Apostolic Fathers is debated and, in some cases, ultimately uncertain. The chronological arrangement given here is based on the content of the writing themselves. *First Clement* is usually considered the first book to have been written after the New Testament. However, the internal evidence within the *Epistle to Diognetus* and the *Didache* suggests that they were written before the generally accepted date of *1 Clement*. Also, there is evidence that Papias wrote early than is usually thought. The dates of the other works are the ones usually given.

1. *The Epistle to Diognetus* (ca. A.D. 100) is an anonymous letter written by a disciple of the Apostles. *The Epistle* has been dated at 117 (Westcott), between 120 and 130 (Ewald), 130 (Roberts-Donaldson), 135 (Otto; Bunsen), about 150 (Lightfoot), and even later in the third century (Zahn; Harnack). The evidence from the Epistle itself suggests an early date, before 100 and possibly before 70. It speaks of Christianity as new (1:1, 2:1). Since the author says he was a disciple of the Apostles (11:1; note the plural), he must have written during or shortly after their lifetime. He also speaks of the Jews making sacrifices with blood and fat and whole burnt offerings (3:5). When the Temple was destroyed in 70, the sacrifices ceased, so this could indicate that the *Epistle to Diognetus* was written before 70. If so, this is the earliest non-canonical Christian writing in existence.

The author writes, "For the scriptures state clearly how God from the beginning planted a tree of life in the midst of paradise" (12:3), a reference to the book of Genesis. He quotes 1 Corinthians 8:1, stating, "the apostle says" (12:5). Many words and phrases in the book are reminiscent of the New Testament. The author refers to "the observance of months and of days" (4:5; *cf.* Gal. 4:10). He calls believers "sojourners" (5:5; *cf.* 1 Pet. 1:1). He says, "their citizenship is in heaven" (5:9; *cf.* Phil. 3:20). When they are reviled, they bless (5:5; *cf.* 1 Pet. 2:23, 39; Mt. 5:11). They are in the world, but not of the world (6:3; *cf.* Jn. 17:13-14). The One who was sent was "gentle and meek" (7:4; *cf.* 2 Cor. 10:1). He was sent as loving, not is judging (7:5; *cf.* Jn. 3:16-17). The Son died "the just for the unjust" (9:2; *cf.* 1 Pet. 3:18). God sent "His only begotten Son" (10:2; Jn. 3:16). God promised the kingdom and will give it to those who love Him (10:2; cf. Jas. 2:5). He says, "You love Him that so loved you before" (10:2; *cf.* 1 Jn. 4:19). Believers are "imitators of God" (10:6; Eph. 5:1) "He sent forth the Word, that He might appear unto the world, who being dishonored by the people, and preached by the Apostles, was believed in by the Gentiles" (11:3; *cf.* 1 Tim. 3:16). The Word was from the beginning (11:4; *cf.* Jn. 1:1). "The apostles say, "Knowledge puffs up, but charity edifies" (12:5; *cf.* 1 Cor. 8:1). In other words, the author knew 1 Corinthians and, no doubt, nine other New Testament books (Jn.; 2 Cor.; Gal.; Eph.; Phil.; 1 Tim.; Titus; Jas.; and 1 Pet.).

Thiessen says the letter contains language resembling 2 Cor. 6:8-10 (ch. v, Thiessen, p. 207), speaks of "observing months and days" as in Galatians 4:10 (ch. iv, Thiessen, p. 213), seems to allude to Philippians 3:20 (ch. v, Thiessen, p. 247), has a possible reminiscence of Titus 3:4 (ch. ix) and of 1 Tim. 3:16 (ch. xi, Thiessen, p. 254) and seems to allude to the idea in 1 John 4:19 (ch. 10, Thiessen, p. 306; Everett Harrison, p. 411).

2. *The Didache* is also known as the *Teaching of the Twelve Apostles*. Although some date the work in the middle of the second century (Harnack dates it after 131; Cairns, in the middle of the second century, p. 77), many have argued for a date before 100. It speaks of apostles and prophets coming to minister (*Didache*, 11:5-9). There is no mention in early literature of apostles later than in the apostolic age. Clement and Ignatius do not even mention itinerant ministers. Moreover, the Didache speaks of the twofold ministries of bishops and deacons (Didache, 15:1-2). Some say it was written between 80-90 (Bartlet; Ehrhard) and others say before 70 (Sabatier; Minasi; Jacquier). Ehrman says it appears to have been written "at the same time as or possibly even earlier than some of the books of the New Testament" (Ehrman, vol. 1, p. 165). Jonathan Zdziarski, a scientist who has studied and translated the Didache, dates it between A.D. 49 and 79 (see www.zdziarski.com/papers/didache. The dating of the Didache at 49 is probably too early, but dating it before 100, even between 80 and 90, is reasonable. (McDonald says it was likely written between A.D. 70 and 120.)

There are quotations and numerous allusions to the *Gospel of Matthew*. For example, the author says, "Neither pray like the hypocrites, but as the Lord has commanded in His Gospel, in this way pray" (*Didache*, 8:2). The author quotes the entire Lord's Prayer, including the ending omitted by the modern Critical Text (*Didache*, 8:2-7). He also states, "The meek will inherit the land" (*Didache*, 3:7). Several times, he mentions being double-minded (*Didache*, 2:4, 4:4), reminiscent of James 1:8. There are allusions to other books of the New Testament, including slaves being told to be subject to their masters *Didache*, 4:11; *cf.* Eph. 6:5; Col. 3:22), believers being told not to eat meat sacrificed to idols (*Didache*, 6:3; *cf.* Acts 15:29), believers being instructed that if people do not work, do not let them live with you idle (*Didache*, 12:4; 2 Thess. 3:11-12), and prophets are worthy of their food as workmen are worthy of theirs (*Didache*, 13:1-2; 1 Tim. 5:17).

The author admonishes his readers: "And reprove one another not in wrath but in peace as you find in the Gospel, and let none speak with any who has done wrong to his neighbor, nor let him hear a word from you until he repents. But your prayers, alms, and all your acts perform as ye find in the Gospel of our Lord" *(Didache*, 15.3-4). Harrison says, "Numerous citations from Matthew are used, but without naming the source" (Everett Harrison, p. 94). Thiessen says, "It uses Matthew a good deal and Luke some" and "it knows most of our New Treatment books" (Thiessen, p. 13).

3. Clement of Rome wrote to the church at Corinth. His letter was written early. It refers to the deaths of Peter and Paul as 'belong[ing] to our generation" (Clement, 5:1-5). On the other hand, it is not too early because it refers to the Corinthian church as "ancient" (Clement, 47:7) and speaks of some members who

had been Christians "from youth to old age" (Clement, 63:3). It should also be noted that 1 Clement was written soon after a period of persecution (Clement, 1:1). If that was the persecution of Nero, the epistle was written about 68. If the persecution referred to was that of Domitian, the epistle was written at the close of the first century or the beginning of the second. A date of about 97 is the one generally accepted.

First Clement contains abundant references to the writings of the New Testament. In one instance, Clement says, "Most of all, remembering the words of our Lord Jesus Christ which He spoke teaching forbearances and longsuffering; for this, He spoke." He then quotes from Christ's Sermon on the Mount (chapter 13; *cf.* Mt. 5:7, 6:14, 15; 7:1, 12, 14; Lk. 16:31, 36-38). Some have argued that he is quoting from oral tradition rather than the written Gospels, but in chapter 46, he again says, "Remember the words of our Lord Jesus for He said," and this time records a saying of Christ recorded in Matthew 18:6, 26:24; Mark 9:42, 14:21, and Luke 17:1, 2. Clement may be quoting Matthew, Mark, Luke, or all three. Lightfoot affirms that Clement used written Gospels (Everett Harrison, p. 93). He uses phraseology from the New Testament, such as telling the Corinthians that they were "more glad to give than to receive" (Acts 20:35) and "ready unto every good work" (chapter 2; *cf.* Titus 3:1) and he calls the apostles like Peter and Paul "pillars" (Gal. 2:9) of the church (chapter 5).

In 1 Clement chapter 2, there is a possible allusion to Galatians 3:1 (*cf.* "an abundant outpouring of the Holy Spirit fell upon all") and in chapter 45 to 2 Timothy 1:3 (*cf.* "pure conscience"). At least twice, he seems to be alluding to the book of Romans. He says, "Of Him (that is, God) is the Lord Jesus, as according to the flesh" (chapter 32; *cf.* Rom. 9:5) and "for they that do these things are hateful to God and not only that do them, but they also that consent to do them" (chapter 35; *cf.* Rom. 1:32).

Clement refers to Ephesians 4:4-6 in chapter 46, saying, "Have we not one God and one Christ and one Spirit of grace that was shed upon us? Is there not one calling in Christ?" Who could doubt that Clement had James 3:1 in mind when he says, "Let the wise display his wisdom not in words, but in good works" (chapter 38)? The same could be said of his use of James 3:16.

Clement borrows from Hebrews on several occasions. Speaking of the Lord Jesus, he says, "Being the brightness of his Majesty is so much greater than angels as He inherited a more excellent name. For so it is written, 'Who made His angels spirits and His ministers a flame of fire,' but of His Son, the Master said thus, 'Thou art My Son; I this day have begotten Thee. Ask of me and I will give Thee the Gentiles for Thine inheritance, and the ends of the earth for Thy Possession.' And again, He said unto Him, 'Sit Thou on My right hand until I make Thine enemies a footstool for Thy feet'" (*cf.* 1 Clement 36 with Heb. 1:2, 3, 4, 6, 13). He says Moses was "a faithful servant in all his house" (*cf.* 1 Clement 43 with Heb. 3:5). In chapter 17, he said, "Let us become imitators also of those who went about in goatskins and sheepskins" (Heb. 11:37).

In chapter 7, there is an allusion to 1 Peter, where Clement says, "Let us fix our eyes on the blood of Christ and understand how precious it is to His Father" (1 Pet. 1:19). In chapter 34, he says, "Since he forewarned us, saying, 'Behold the Lord and His reward is before His face to recompense each man according to his work" (Rev. 22:12).

While some of these references in 1 Clement are mere allusions to the New Testament, there can be absolutely no doubt that he knew about 1 Corinthians. In chapter 47, he said, "Take up the epistle of the blessed Paul the apostle. What wrote he first unto you in the beginning of the gospel? Of a truth, he charged you in the Spirit concerning himself and Cephas and Apollos because that even then ye had made parties." Is there not a reference to 2 Corinthians 13:8 in Clement's statement, "Through Him let us look steadfastly into the heights of the heavens. Through Him, we behold as in a mirror His faultless and most excellent visage?" (chapter 36).

There is no question that Clement was familiar with the writings of the New Testament. He either quotes or alludes to Matthew, Mark, Luke, Acts, Romans, 1 and 2 Corinthians, Galatians, Ephesians, 2 Timothy, Titus, Hebrews, James, 1 Peter, and the book of Revelation. Moreover, Clement wrote, "Take up the epistle of the blessed Apostle Paul. What did he write to you at the time when the Gospel first began to be preached? Truly, under the inspiration of the Spirit, he wrote to you concerning himself, and Cephas, and Apollos, because even then parties had been formed among you" (1 Clement 47:1-3). Clement of Rome said Paul wrote to the Corinthians "under the inspiration of the Spirit!"

4. Papias was a leader in the church of Hierapolis in Phrygia, about 100 miles east of Ephesus. According to Irenaeus, he was "the hearer of John and a companion of Polycarp" (Irenaeus, *Ag. Her.* 5.33.4). Scholars disagree concerning the date for Papias. In an article entitled "The Date of Papias: A Reassessment," Robert W. Yarborough lists the reasons for a late date and gives the evidence for an early date (Yarborough, *JETS*, volume 26, pp. 181-82). Yarborough argues that Papias is likely to have written ca. 95-110.

Papias was the author of five books entitled the *Interpretations of the Sayings of the Lord*, which unfortunately have disappeared, except for a few fragments that are recorded in the writings of Irenaeus (Papias, *Against Heresies*, 5:33.4, 5:36.1-2) and Eusebius (Eusebius, *Eccl. Hist.*, 3:39.3-5, 15-16; see 3:24 for Eusebius' view). The Eusebius section says Matthew wrote his work in Hebrew, and Mark was Peter's interpreter (Cairns, p. 76). Papias mentions Matthew and Mark, quotes 1 John and 1 Peter, and knows John's gospel (Thiessen, p. 13). According to Yarborough, the implications of the early date are 1) another voice, perhaps the earliest, to the early authorship and circulation of 1 John and 1 Peter (Eusebius, *Eccl. Hist.*, 3.39. 17); 2) verification of the tradition of the aged apostle John's ministry in Asia Minor (Eusebius, *Eccl. Hist.*, 3.39.3-4); 3) an indication that Mark's Gospel comprises Peter's preaching (Eusebius, *Eccl. Hist.*, 3.39.15); and 4) an indication that Matthew wrote a gospel in Hebrew (G. Kittel, "Logion," TDNT vol. 4, pp. 140-141). To that list, could be added that most agree Papias refers to the story of the woman taken in adultery (Morris in his commentary on the Gospel of John, p. 883; he cites Eusebius, *Eccl. Hist.*, 3:39, 17).

5. Polycarp (A.D. 69-155) was Bishop of Smyrna. He wrote a letter to the Philippians about A.D. 110 (Cairns, p. 75) and was burned at the stake in A.D. 155 at age 86 (Cairns, pp. 74-75). According to his pupil, Irenaeus, Polycarp was a student of John the Apostle. Polycarp's epistle (ca. A.D. 110) contains about sixty quotations from the New Testament, thirty-four of which are from the writings of Paul (Cairns, p. 75). He refers to Paul being at Philippi and writing them a letter (chapter 2). To be more specific, he quotes 14 books of the New Testament, including Matthew, Luke, Acts, Romans, 1 Corinthians, Galatians, Ephesians, Philippians, 1 Timothy, 2 Timothy, 1 Thessalonians, 2 Thessalonians, 1 Peter, and 1 John (Thiel claims that Polycarp alludes to all 27 books of the NT; for his proof see www.COGwriter.com).

Harrison says his letter to the Philippians, which he dates ca. 115, "abounds with language drawn from the New Testament. More than once, statements are attributed to Jesus, introduced by the words, 'The Lord said.' In citing Paul, Polycarp several times uses the introductory phrase, 'knowing that,' which Lightfoot takes to be a formula of citation (see 1:15; 5:1). Most striking is the quoting of Psalm 4:5, 'Be angry and sin not,' followed immediately by Ephesians 4:26, 'Let not the sun go down upon your wrath,' and the prefacing of the combined statements with the words, 'as it is said in these Scriptures' (12: 1)" (Everett Harrison, p. 94). McDonald says, "Polycarp appears to have consciously placed an OT Scripture and a Christian writing on an equal authoritative footing" (McDonald, p. 276). Kistemaker concurs, saying, "Polycarp considers Paul's letter to the Ephesians Scripture and to be equal to the OT" (Kistemaker, p. 8).

6. Ignatius was from Antioch in Syria and wrote seven letters about A.D. 110 (Cairns, p. 74; McDonald dates him ca. A.D. 100-107, p. 275). There are two versions of his writings; one is shorter than the other. Ignatius quotes Matthew 13:33 (Eph. 14), 1 Cor. 6:9-10 (Eph. 16), 2 Cor. 4:18 (Rom. 3), and 1 Thess. 5:17 (Polycarp 1). In Ephesians 5, he quotes, "God resists the proud" (Prov. 3:34; Jas. 4:6; 1 Pet. 5:5). He alludes to Matthew 18:19 (Eph. 5), 1 Pet. 2:5 (Eph. 9), and John 12:7 (Eph. 17). Writing to the Ephesians, Ignatius uses phrases from the New Testament book of Ephesians (*cf.* his Eph. 1 with Eph. 5:2). In addition, in the longer version, he quotes Colossians 2:10 and 1 Timothy 4:10 (Eph. 8); John 14:6, (Eph. 9); 2 Tim. 2:24-25 (Eph. 10); 1 Pet. 2:23 (Eph. 10); Luke 23:34 (Eph. 10); Ephesians 6:12 (Eph. 13); Romans 10:10 (Eph. 15); 2 Cor. 6:14-16 (Eph. 14); 1 Cor. 1:18 (Eph. 18); Luke 6:46 (Magnesians 4); John 5:30 (Magnesians 7); 2 Thess. 3:10 (Magnesians 9). He also says Paul wrote to the Ephesians (Eph. 6). Ignatius knew the New Testament in general, especially the epistles of Paul, but Matthew and the Gospel of John are his favorites (Thiessen, p. 12). He "carefully distinguishes his own position from that of the apostles" (Everett Harrison, p. 94).

7. Quadratus was one of the first Christian apologists. Jerome said that Quadratus represents an apology (a defense of Christianity) to Hadrian. Hadrian reigned as Emperor of Rome from 117 to 138. Eusebius quotes Quadratus as saying that some

who were healed were still alive, which would probably put his date closer to 117 than 138. The only surviving writing of Quadratus is a short passage recorded by Eusebius. It does not contain any quotations from Scripture, but it does say, "The works of our Savior were always present, for they were genuine: those that were healed, and those that were raised from the dead, who were seen not only when they were healed and when they were raised but were also always present; and not merely while the Savior was on earth, but also after his death, they were alive for quite a while, so that some of them lived even to our day" (Eusebius, *Hist. Eccl.* 4.1-2).

8. *The Epistle of Barnabas* was not written by the New Testament person by that name. It was written about A.D. 130 (Cairns p. 75; McDonald dates him ca. A.D. 90-130, p. 274). While there are numerous references to the Old Testament, there are only a few to the New Testament. In chapter 4, the author says, "as it is written, 'Many are called, but few were chosen'" (Mt. 20:16 or 22:14). This statement is introduced by a formula that is common for the quotation of Old Testament Scripture— 'as it stands written' (*The Epistle of Barnabas*, 4:14)" (Everett Harrison, p. 93; see also McDonald, p. 275). In chapter 5, he says, "He came not to call the righteous, but sinners to repentance" (Mt. 9:13; Mk. 2:17; Lk. 5:32). In chapter 7, he writes, "The Lord says, 'Behold, I will make the last like the first'" (Mt. 20:16). There is a possible allusion to Colossians 1:16 (Barnabas 11). Thiessen says, "It quotes Matthew and there are echoes of Romans, 1 and 2 Corinthians, and Ephesians. The writer perhaps knew 1 Peter and

certain passages reminded us of John" (Thiessen, p. 17).

9. *The Shepherd of Hermas* is an apocalypse (*cf.* Daniel and Revelation). The earliest mention of The Shepherd is in the Muratorian Fragment. It says Hermas "composed the Shepherd very late in our time in the city of Rome, while Bishop Pius, his brother, occupied the chair of the Roman Church." Pius is dated ca. 141-157 (Thiessen, p. 21). The Shepherd was probably written about 150 (Cairns, p. 76). The Shepherd does not contain definite Old or New Testament quotations. Westcott says that the author's knowledge of the New Testament can only be shown "by passing coincidences of language" but acknowledges that those occur throughout the work (Westcott p. 201). Thiessen, however, says it "seems clear" Hermas knew Matthew, Ephesians, Revelation, and maybe Hebrews and James (Thiessen, p. 22).

10. *Second Clement* is an anonymous sermon. He quotes Isaiah 29:13 (2 Clem. 3:5), Isaiah 54:1 (2 Clem. 2:1), Ezekiel 14:14, 20, calling it Scripture (2 Clem. 6:8), Matthew 7:21 (2 Clem. 4:2), Matthew 7:23 (2 Clem. 4:5; see Lk. 13: 26-27), Matthew 9:13, calling it Scripture (2 Clem. 2:4), Matthew 10:16 (2 Clem. 5:2), Matthew 10:32-33 (2 Clem. 3:2), Matthew 12:50 (2 Clem. 9:11), Matthew 16:26 (2 Clem. 6:2), Matthew 21:13, calling it Scripture (2 Clem. 14:1), Mark 9:44 (2 Clem. 17:5), Luke 12:4 (2 Clem. 5:4), Luke 16:13 (2 Clem. 6:1), Luke 1610 (8:5), 1 Corinthians 2:9 (2 Clem. 11:7) and alludes to 1 Corinthians 9:24-27 (2 Clem. 7:5) and 2 Peter 3:10 (2 Clem. 16:3). He also quotes the *Gospel of Peter* and the *Gospel of Thomas* (Ehrman, vol. 2, pp. 50-52).

To sum up, the canon *per se* was not discussed during this period, but the writings that were produced *immediately* after the close of the New Testament A.D. 95-110) quote or allude to every book of the New Testament. Clement of Rome (A.D. 95) calls 1 Corinthians inspired. Papias (A.D. 95-110) wrote an *Exposition of the Oracles of the Lord* (that is, Scripture). He mentions Matthew and Mark, quotes 1 John and 1 Peter and knows John's gospel. Polycarp (A.D. 110) quotes 14 books of the New Testament and considers Paul's letter to the Ephesians Scripture to be equal to the Old Testament. Ignatius (A.D. 110) carefully distinguished himself from the apostles, knew Matthew and John, the New Testament in general, and the epistles of Paul. The author of *The Didache* (ca. A.D. 120) knew most of our New Testament books. *The Epistle of Barnabas* (A.D. 130) quotes Matthew as Scripture.

Kistemaker concludes, "Clement of Rome, Ignatius, Polycarp, and others did not hesitate to accept the letters of Paul and regard them as Scripture. Donald Hagnet notes, 'The Apostolic Fathers are essentially united in their witness to the authority of the new writings; there is no radical change in the valuation of these writings between A.D. 95 and A.D. 140'" (Kistemaker, p. 8).

It is also important to note that the men who wrote immediately after the close of the New Testament did not claim to write Scripture. Kistemaker observes, "Clement of Rome says that his own letter has been 'written through the Holy Spirit' (1 Clem. 63:2). Near the end of the second century, he is referred to as the "apostle Clement" by Clement of Alexandria. And Eusebius, commenting on Clement's letter, says that it enjoyed recognition in the churches because in earlier times, as well as his own, it was read publicly in the assemblies Church History, 3:15–16. 1 Clement, however, is not listed as Scripture in sub-apostolic times. This is rather remarkable in view of the fact that both John's Revelation and Clement's first epistle were written in A.D. 95. Revelation is part of the NT canon; 1 Clement is not. Irenaeus held 1 Clement in high esteem without granting it any status. Except for its inclusion in Codex Alexandrinus, a document of the fifth century, 1 Clement has never been accepted as canonical" (Kistemaker, p. 7).

Kistemaker also says, "Do the apostolic fathers place themselves on a level with the writers of the NT? The answer must be negative. Clement of Rome, Ignatius, and Polycarp do not claim divine authority for themselves. Ignatius speaks with authority when he addresses the churches in his letters. However, he does not put himself in the same category as the apostles. In his letter to the Romans, he writes: "I do not order you as did Peter and Paul; they were Apostles, I am a convict" (4:3; tr. Kirsopp Lake). Also, in his letter to the Trallians, Ignatius deprecates himself: "I am sparing you in my love, though I might write more sharply on his behalf: I did not think myself competent, as a convict, to give orders like an Apostle" (3:3; tr. Kirsopp Lake) (Kistemaker, p. 10).

The Last Half of the Second Century

By A.D. 140 or A.D. 150, all who could have known the apostles had passed off the scene. During the last half of the second century, apostolic Christianity was challenged and Christian apologists defended Christianity.

1   The *Gospel of Truth* was written around A.D. 140 (Everett Harrison, p. 95). Ancient authors mention it, but in 1945, a copy of it was discovered in Egypt (it was one of the Nag Hammadi documents). Irenaeus says the *Gospel of Truth* is a manifesto of the Valentinian school (Irenaeus, *Against Heresies*, 3.11.9). W. C. van Unnik says, "About A.D. 140-150 a collection of writings was known at Rome and accepted as authoritative which was virtually identical with our New Testament" (cited by Bruce, CS, p. 147). Bruce, who does not subscribe to the conclusion of Unnik, says, "The treatise alludes to Matthew and Luke (possibly with Acts), the gospel and first letter of John, the Pauline letters (except the Pastorals), Hebrews and Revelation-and not only alludes to them but cites them in terms which presuppose that they are authoritative" (Bruce, CS, p. 147).

McDonald states, "Some awareness of a collection of writings may have been known earlier than the time of Marcion. Tertullian states that Valentinus (ca. 135-160), in contrast to Marcion, used all the Scriptures and perverted them: 'One man perverts the Scriptures with his hand, another their meaning by his exposition. For although Valentinus seems to uses the entire volume has none the less laid violent hands on the truth only with a more cunning mind and skill than Marcion. Marcion expressly and openly used the knife, not the pen, since he made such an excision of the Scripture as suited his own subject matter. Valentinus, however, abstained from such excision because he did not invent Scriptures to square with his own subject matter but adapted his matter to the Scriptures; and yet he took away more and added more by removing the proper meaning of every particular word and adding fantastic arrangements of things which had no real existence (*Praescr,* 38.4-6)'" (McDonald, p. 308).

McDonald says, "The phrase *entire volume* appears to refer to a collection of Scriptures, probably the NT writings, but possibly the OT Scriptures as well. The context favors the former since Tertullian asks both Marcion and Valentinus what right they have to use the Scripture received from the Apostles *(Praescr,* 32), which could not, of course, refer to the OT writings" (McDonald, p. 308). McDonald adds, "Tertullian evidently believed that Valentinus used a collection of NT writings similar to his own" (McDonald, pp. 308-309).

2. Marcion (ca. A.D. 140, Cairns, p. 99) was a wealthy member of the church in Rome. He rejected the God and the Scriptures of the Jews and set up his own canon, which consisted of the Gospel of Luke and ten letters of Paul. He may have been one of the first to call one of the canonical Gospels a "gospel" (McDonald, p. 325). He did not believe that Jesus entered human life by being born of a woman (Bruce, CS, p. 136). He founded his own church when he was expelled from the Roman church. His church eventually died out because celibacy was required (Bruce, CS, p. 136).

According to Adolf von Harnack, Marcion established the first canon (McDonald, p. 326). In Harnack's opinion, in reaction to Marcion and other second-century heretics, Christians were motivated to identify their sacred Scriptures (Everett Harrison, p. 108; McDonald, p. 323; for the other heretics, see Sheeley, p. 517). Marcion forced the hand of the church when he set up his own canon. The church corrected him by adding more books to his small collection.

The church did not formulate a canon as a reaction to Marcion. Scholars today reject Harnack's theory (McDonald, p. xix). Granted, Marcion's canon produced a violent reaction in the church. Irenaeus attacked him, and Tertullian wrote five books against him but the canon of Marcion demonstrates: 1) the books he accepted were regarded as "indisputably authentic," and 2) the books he rejected were "accepted as canonical by the masses at large" (Tenney, p. 424).

Harrison says, "Before Marcion's time, there is reasonably clear evidence of the Gospel canon and a collection of Paul's writings" (Everett Harrison, p. 108, who points to the use of the word "Scripture" and the formulas by which Scripture was commonly introduced, for example, in Barnabas 4:14, 2 Clement 2:4, Polycarp, Philippians chapter 12; see also the discussion about Valentinus above). Harrison adds, "Tertullian and other Fathers charge Marcion with rejecting books. This in itself presupposes in the minds of these men the acknowledged position of such books in what was in fact a canon, even though it had not been published as such" (Everett Harrison, pp. 108-109). Bruce says that in light of the Nag Hammadi document, it can be argued that Marcion's canon was "his revision of an existing canon of the New

Testament writings" (Bruce, p. 148).

Bruce contends that in the debate with the Valentinians, Marcion, and others, the issue was the interpretation of the Bible. He goes on to say that the church leaders, in essence, said, "We do not reject the Old Testament scriptures, as Marcion does; we accept them, as did Jesus and the apostles (both the original apostles and Paul). As for the scriptures of the new order, we accept not one gospel writing only, but four (including the complete text of Marcion's mutilated *Gospel*). We accept not only ten letters of Paul, but thirteen (that is, including the three addressed to Timothy and Titus). We accept not the letters of Paul only, but letters of other apostles too. And we accept the Acts of the Apostles, a work which links the gospels and the apostolic letters, providing the sequel to the former and the background to the latter" (Bruce, CS, p. 151).

3. *The Shepherd of Hermas* was probably written about A.D. 150 (Cairns, p. 76). Harrison says it "shows acquaintance with the teaching of the Gospels and with several of the Epistles, but there is no citation of any of this material as Scripture" (Everett Harrison, p. 94).

4. *Second Clement* (ca. A.D. 150, Cairns, p. 75; McDonald dates him ca. A.D. 120-140, but no later than A.D. 140, p. 274) quotes Isaiah 41:1 and says, "and another Scripture, however, says, 'I came not to call the righteous, but sinners'" (*2 Clem.* 2:5), a quotation from Matthew 9:13. Thus, the author of 2 Clement calls Matthew Scripture. It introduces a saying of Jesus from Luke 16:10-12 with the words, "For the Lord says in the Gospel"

(*2 Clem.* 8.5). For a list of the similarities between the Synoptic Gospels, see McDonald, p. 256, fn. 43.

5. Ptolemy (ca. A.D. 160, McDonald, p. 277), Valentinus's principal disciple and probably his successor (Bruce, CS, p. 148), wrote *Letter to Flora*. In it, he appeals to the words (3:5, 3:8, 4:1, 4:4), commands of the Savior (5:10), and teaching of Jesus (7:9). He quotes John 1:3 with the phrase "the apostle says" (3:6). He cites Paul as one would quote Scripture. McDonald says, "These references are especially meaningful since Ptolemy comes outside mainstream orthodox Christianity" (McDonald, p. 278).

Here are quotations from *Letter to Flora* with the references to the New Testament added: "Such persons do not comprehend what was said by the Savior. For a house or city divided against itself cannot stand [Matt. 12:25], declared our Savior. Furthermore, the apostle says that the creation of the world is due to him, for everything was made through him, and apart from him, nothing was made [John 1:3]. In some discussion with those who dispute with the Savior about divorce, which was permitted in the Law, he said Because of your hard-heartedness Moses permitted a man to divorce his wife; from the beginning, it was not so; for God made this marriage, and what the Lord joined together, man must not separate [Matt. 19:8]. The Savior also makes plain the fact that there are some traditions of the elders interwoven in the Law. For God, he says, Said, Honor your father and your mother, that it may be well with you, But you, he says addressing the elders, ...have declared as a gift to God, that by which you have nullified the Law of God through the tradition of your elders. Isaiah also proclaimed this, saying, This people honors me with their lips, but their hearts are far from me, teaching precepts which are the commandments of men [Matt. 15:4-9]. Called Law, which the Savior came not to destroy but to complete [Matt. 5:17]. Paul the apostle shows that the Passover and the unleavened bread are images when he says, Christ, our Passover has been sacrificed, in order that you may be unleavened bread, not containing leaven (by leaven he here means evil), but may be a new lump [1 Cor. 5:7]. The disciples of the Savior and the Apostle Paul showed that this theory is true, speaking of the part dealing with images, as we have already said, in mentioning The Passover for us and the Unleavened bread, for the law interwoven with injustice when he says that the law of commandments in ordinances were destroyed [Eph. 2:15]; and of that not mixed with anything inferior when he says that The law is holy, and the commandment is holy and just and good [Rom. 7:12]. There is only one ungenerated Father, from whom are all things" [1 Cor. 8:6].

6. Justin Martyr (ca. A.D. 100-165) was the foremost Christian apologist of the second century (Cairns, p. 76; McDonald says Justin wrote ca. A.D. 150-160, McDonald, p. 289). He wrote two *Apologies* and *Dialogue with Trypho the Jew*. Miller says that Justin Martyr "quotes copiously from the New Testament" (Miller cited by Baker, p. 84).

In his *First Apology*, he says, "On the day called Sunday, all Christians gather together to one place and the memoirs of the apostles or the writings of the prophets are read as long as time permits, and when the reader has ceased, the president verbally instructs and exhorts to the imitation of these good things. Then we all rise together and pray, and as we said before, when our prayer is ended, bread and wine and water are brought, and the president in like manner offers prayers and thanksgivings, according to his ability, and the people assent, saying 'Amen.'" (*First Apology*, chapter 67). In a preceding chapter, "the memoirs of the apostles" are also called Gospels (See *First Apology*, chapter 63:3). Harrison argues that it is probable that the memoirs of the apostles are the same as our canonical gospels because "there is substantial agreement between Justin's allusions to items in the life of Christ and the corresponding material in our Gospels," "when Justin refers to traditions not found in Gospels, he does not cite gospel authority for them" and "six times he uses the formula 'it is written' in connection with the Gospels, but not in connection with the items derived from other sources" (Everett Harrison, p. 96). McDonald concurs, saying Justin probably knew all four canonical gospels (McDonald, p. 265), and for Justin, the canonical Gospels functioned equally to the Old Testament (McDonald, p. 286).

Justin refers to Matthew 11:27 with the Scripture-like designation, "It is written" (*Dialogue*, 100.1; McDonald, p. 285). He states that the book of Revelation was the work of "a certain man among us whose name was John, one of the apostles of Christ" (*Dialogue* 81) and calls it one of "our writings" (*First Apology*, 28:1). He also remarks, "No Scripture contradicts another" (*Dialogue*, 65.2). McDonald claims Justin is the first orthodox writer to set forth a doctrine of Scripture (McDonald,

p. 286).

7. Tatian (ca. A.D. 110-172), a pupil of Justin, wrote *Addresses to the Greeks* and composed the *Diatessaron* (A.D. 170, Thiessen; 173-175; McDonald, p. 293), the earliest harmony of the Gospels (Cairns, p. 107). Diatessaron means "through four." Beginning with John 1:1, the *Diatessaron* places the Gospel materials in a continuous narrative, omitting parallel passages.

Harrison points out that Eusebius (ca. A.D. 265-339, Cairns, p. 143) says Tatian "composed in some way a combination and collection of the Gospels, and gave this the name of the *Diatessaron*, and this is still extant in some places." Epiphanius explicitly affirms the presence of the four Gospels in this work (A.D. 315-404). In the fifth century, Theodoret (A.D. 393-457) reports having found over 200 such books in the churches of Syria, which he ordered replaced by the Gospels of the Four Evangelists (Everett Harrison, p. 97). The point is that ca. A.D. 170, the four Gospels were accepted as canonical. Thiessen says Tatian knew the four Gospels and nearly all of our New Testament books (Thiessen, p. 21).

8. The Muratorian Fragment (A.D. 170) gets its name from Muratori, who discovered it in the Ambrosian Library in Milan. The great debate is over the date of its composition. The traditional date is that it was written at the end of the second century or the beginning of the third, making it the earliest known canon list, "one that has the same 'core' of writings which were later agreed upon by the whole church" (Hill, p. 437). In his book, *The Muratorian Fragment and the Development of the Canon*,

Hahneman argues for a fourth-century date. For a refutation of Hahneman and a defense of the consensus view, see the article in the *Westminster Theological Journal* by C. E. Hill entitled, "The Debate over the Muratorian Fragment and the Development of the Canon."

The Muratorian manuscript is mutilated at the beginning. It begins in the middle of a sentence, and the first book mentioned is Luke, which the fragment calls the third Gospel. It is generally assumed that Matthew and Mark are the first two gospels that are missing. John is listed after Luke with an unmistakable reference to the First Epistle. Acts, 1 and 2 Corinthians, Ephesians, Philippians, Colossians, Galatians, 1 and 2 Thessalonians, Romans, Philemon, Titus, 1 and 2 Timothy, Jude, 2 and 3 John, and Revelation were also included. The anonymous author rejects the epistles of Paul to the Laodiceans and to the Alexandrians. He put the Revelation of Peter in the "acknowledged" class, but he is dubious about it, saying, "Some of you do not think that it should be read publicly in the church." He did not mention James or Hebrews, nor the Petrine epistles. The manuscript ends abruptly.

Harrison says, "It is reasonably certain that the list of New Testament books contained herein was drawn up in conscious opposition to the canon of the heretic Marcion, whose theological views were unacceptable to the church at Rome. Marcion's heresy is referred to by name, and the description of the Gospels as a whole—"all things in all (of them) are declared by the one sovereign Spirit"—suggests a side glance at Marcion with his deliberate choice of Luke to the exclusion of the other three"

(Everett Harrison, p. 97).

Harrison says, "In the Muratorian Canon, the opening words apparently have to do with Mark (the portion dealing with Matthew is lost). Then Luke and John are mentioned, followed by the Acts, then the thirteen epistles of Paul, beginning with I Corinthians and concluding with the two to Timothy. Pseudo-Pauline letters to the Laodiceans and to the Alexandrians are mentioned but not as accepted. The list is rounded out by the Epistle of Jude, two of John, also his Apocalypse, with the indication that some accept that of Peter, but others will not have it read in the church. Some scholars have felt that the text is corrupt here and originally indicated one epistle (rather than Apocalypse) of Peter as accepted, with doubt cast on the second epistle. If this critical emendation be accepted, only Hebrews, James, and one epistle of John are absent. As Westcott notes, the Muratorian Canon is not an individualistic document, the statement of a personal opinion or the expression of a novel theory, but a deliberate exposition of the views of the church universal so far as the writer is acquainted with its outlook and practice" (Everett Harrison, p. 98).

Ryrie says the Muratorian canon "omitted Hebrews, James, and 1 and 2 Peter. However, there is a break in the manuscript, so we cannot be certain that these books were not included. This canon also rejects some other books like the Shepherd of Hermas, which did not become part of the canon" (Ryrie, p. 109).

Hill concludes, "With or without the MF, there is ample evidence that the church was operating with a conception of a closed canon at least by the latter half of the second century." He goes on to explain that writers like Irenaeus (Irenaeus, *Ag. Her.* 3.1.1) and Serapion (Serapion, *Hist. Eccl.* 6.12.3–6) speak of the New Testament writings as those that were "passed on" to them from the previous generation (Hill. pp. 451-452).

9. *Martyrs of Lyons and Vienne* (ca. 175-177, McDonald, p. 278) is a letter preserved by Eusebius (*Eccl. Hist.* 5.1). It contains many references, allusions, and quotations from the New Testament, including a reference to Revelation 22:11, which is preceded by "that the Scripture might be fulfilled" (*Eccl. Hist.* 5.1.58). This is one of the earliest references to the book of Revelation as "Scripture" (McDonald, p. 278).

10. Athenagoras (ca. A.D. 180, McDonald, p. 279) says, "The result of all of this is very plain to everyone, namely, that, in the language of the apostle 'This corruptible must put on incorruption' [1 Cor. 15:54], so that those who were dead ... may, in accordance with justice, 'receive what he has done by the body, whether it be good or bad'" [2 Cor. 5:10] (Athenagoras, *Resurrection of the Dead*, 18).

11. Theophilus of Antioch (ca. A.D. 190-200, McDonald, p. 279) shows "heavy dependence" upon the writings of Paul and calls Romans 2:7-9 and 1 Corinthians 2:9 "prophetic Scriptures" (McDonald, p. 297). For example, he writes, "But you also, please give reverential attention to the prophetic Scriptures, for they will make it plain to you how to escape the eternal punishments and obtain the eternal prizes of God. For He who gave the mouth for speech, and formed the ear to hear and made the eye to see will examine all things and will judge [with] righteous judgment. [He

will also] render merited awards for those who seek immortality, and He will give life everlasting, joy, peace, rest, and abundance of good things, which neither has the eye seen nor ear heard nor has it entered into the heart of man to conceive. But to the unbelieving and despisers, who do not obey the truth but are obedient to adulteries and fornications, and filthiness, and covetousness, and unlawful idolatries, there shall be anger and wrath, tribulation and anguish, and at last, an everlasting fire shall possess them" (Theophilus, *Autol.* 1.14).

12. Irenaeus (b. ca. A.D. 115-ca. 200; Farnell, pp. 53-86) was from Smyrna, where he sat at the feet of Polycarp, who was privileged to have personal contact with several "eyewitnesses of the Word of life" (Eusebius, *Eccl. Hist.* V. xx. 6). In his *Epistle to Florinus,* Irenaeus mentions the instruction he had received as a boy from Polycarp and states that this venerable figure "reported all things in agreement with the Scripture" (*Eusebius, HE* V. xx. 6). He says the Scriptures are "perfect since they were spoken by the Word of God and His Spirit" (*Haer.* 2.28.2). Irenaeus wrote *Against Heresies* about A.D. 185 (Cairns, p. 110; McDonald says his writings were ca. A.D. 170-180, p. 289).

Irenaeus distinguishes "the writings of truth" from the "multitude of apocryphal and spurious writings" (Irenaeus, *Against Heresies* 3.21.2). He criticizes Marcion for only accepting Luke and some of the epistles of Paul, which indicates that he not only accepted those books but others as well (Tenney, p. 423).

Nowhere in the extant writing of Irenaeus is there a list of New Testament books, "but it is evident that he had a clear notion of their identity" (Bruce, CS, p. 173). He does not list the letters of Paul, "but he evidently accepted the whole corpus of thirteen letters; the only letter he does not mention is the short letter to Philemon, which he had no occasion to cite" (Bruce, CS, p. 176).

Irenaeus declares that there are four gospels and no more than four. He says, "The Word ... gave to us the Gospel in a fourfold shape, but held together by one Spirit" (Irenaeus, *Against Heresies* III. xi. 8). McDonald says Irenaeus is the first to promote a fixed four-gospel canon (McDonald, p. 289) and he may be the first to designate Christian writings as "New Testament" (McDonald, p. 290; he also says Melito appears to have done so at roughly the same time).

Harrison comments, "In the same passage, Irenaeus gives several reasons why there are four Gospels. But these reasons, however fanciful and mystical—such as the existence of four directions and four winds—are not the actual grounds upon which he receives four Gospels and no more, but a justification for the existence of these only as given by God" (Everett Harrison, p. 99). McDonald comments, "Irenaeus argued that the four canonical Gospels and other unspecified NT literature, along with an unspecified collection of OT writings, were the normative Scriptures for the churches, and he unambiguously called these writings 'Scripture' (see Irenaeus, Haer. 1.9.4; 2.26.1-2; 3.1.1). Although Irenaeus promotes the necessity and authority of the four canonical Evangelists, 'these four and no more,' he also argues for something that no one before him claimed: the Christian message was somehow incomplete if less than four Gospels were used to articulate the Christian faith" (McDonald, p. 290).

Miller says Irenaeus makes 1800 quotations from the New Testament and recognizes the four Gospels, Acts, 13 Pauline epistles, 1 Peter, 1 John, and Revelation as canonical Scripture (Miller, cited by Baker, p. 84). Harrison argues that a lack of mention of a few books is not proof of their non-canonical standing in the eyes of Irenaeus since he does not furnish a formal list of New Testament writings (Everett Harrison, pp. 99-100). Thus, Irenaeus accepted the Old and New Testaments as Scripture (McDonald, p. 296). The fact that Irenaeus appears to acknowledge the authority of the *Shepherd of Hermas* and 1 Clement may prove nothing "since he was writing to address specific issues (heresy), and he would naturally utilize the writings that best suited his argument" (McDonald, p. 301).

13. Clement of Alexandria (ca. A.D. 150-215, McDonald, p. 301) wrote explanations of all the canonical Scriptures, including the disputed writings, and even commented on the Epistle of Barnabas and the Apocalypse of Peter. "He was clear, however, in his understanding of the line between canonical and apocryphal with respect to the Gospels. After quoting a saying of an apocryphal nature, he says, 'We do not find this saying in the four Gospels that have been handed down to us, but in that according to the Egyptians'" (Cement of Alexandria, *Miscellanies* III, xiii, Everett Harrison, p. 100).

"Clement refers to or cites as Scripture many of the writings of the NT: the four canonical Gospels, Acts, fourteen Letters of Paul (the Pastorals and Hebrews were attributed to Paul), 1-2 John,

1 Peter, Jude, and Revelation. He makes no mention of James, 2 Peter, or 3 John. He also quotes from *Barnabas, 1 Clement, Shepherd of Hermas, Preaching of Peter, Sibylline Oracles*, and the *Didache* for support of his ideas" (McDonald, p. 302).

14. Tertullian (A.D. 160-225, McDonald, p. 303; his writings are from A.D. 196-212, Bruce, CS, p. 180) refuses to use any other Gospels than those that the church acknowledges as inspired and authoritative. In a single passage, he mentions Corinthians, Galatians, Philippians, Thessalonians, Ephesians, and Romans as samples of apostolic writings (Tertullian, *Against Marcion*, IV.5). "Concerning some of the Catholic Epistles, he is silent" (Everett Harrison, p. 100). He cites or quotes the four canonical Gospels, thirteen letters of Paul, Acts, 1 John, 1 Peter, Jude, and Revelation and on one occasion, he refers to them as an "entire volume" (*Praescr.* 32). He also says that the Roman church "mingles the Law and the prophets in one volume" (*Praescr.* 32, McDonald, p. 304).

Tertullian says the *Shepherd of Hermas* had been "habitually judged by every council of churches ... among apocryphal and false (writings)." This comment indicates that discussions on the canon may have been fairly common in some areas.

Bruce says while Tertullian did not formally enumerate the contents of a canon, he "approved of the idea which 'canon' later came to express." His canon "certainly comprised the four gospels and Acts, the thirteen epistles which bear Paul's name, 1 Peter, 1 John and Revelation (which he ascribes to John the apostle). It also included the epistle of Jude, which he ascribes to the apostle of that name" (Bruce, CS, p. 182).

To sum up, the canon was discussed during this period, and evidence indicates that a New Testament canon existed. *The Gospel of Truth*'s (A.D. 140) reference to the "entire volume" indicates there was a New Treatment canon in A.D. 140. It "corresponded very closely with what we have today" (Everett Harrison, p. 95). Marcion's canon (A.D. 140) demonstrates that the books he accepted were regarded as "indisputably authentic," and the books he rejected were "accepted as canonical by the masses at large" (Tenney, p. 424). *Second Clement* (ca. A.D. 150) calls Matthew Scripture and introduces a saying of Jesus from Luke 16:10-12 with the words, "For the Lord says in the Gospel" (*2 Clem.* 8.5). Justin Martyr (A.D. 160) says, "No Scripture contradicts another" (*Dialogue*, 65.2). Tatian (A.D. 170), a pupil of Justin, composed the *Diatessaron*, a harmony of the four Gospels. The *Muratorian Fragment* (A.D. 170) contains the oldest known list of books of the **New Testament**. It lists all the works accepted as canonical by the churches known to its anonymous author. It lists all the books in the New Testament except Hebrews, James, and 1 and 2 Peter, which may be due to a break in the manuscript, so we cannot be certain that these books were not included. Irenaeus (A.D. 185) declares there are only four Gospels. Tertullian (A.D. 197) cites or quotes the four canonical Gospels, thirteen letters of Paul, Acts, 1 John, 1 Peter, Jude, and Revelation and on one occasion, he refers to them as an "entire volume" (*Praescr.* 32). He says that Rome "mingles the Law and the prophets in one volume" (*Praescr.* 32) and indicates that discussions on the canon may have been fairly common in some areas.

Summary: By A.D. 170, virtually all, if not all, of the books of the New Testament were recognized as Scripture.

"It is remarkable that in the comparatively few writings of that age which have come down to us, so many references can be found to the New Testament books" (Miller cited by Baker, p. 84).

A clear indication is that only the four Gospels of Matthew, Mark, Luke, and John were recognized as Scripture by A.D. 170. In his book *Against Heresies*, written about A.D. 180, Irenaeus, referring to them by name, says, "As there are four quarters of the world in which we live and four universal winds, and as the Church is dispersed over all the earth, the gospel is the pillar and base of the Church and the breath of life, so it is natural that it should have four pillars, breathing immortality from every quarter and kindling life of men anew. Whence it is manifest that the Word, the architect of all things, who sits upon the cherubim and holds all things together, having been manifested to men, has given us the gospel in fourfold force, but held together by one Spirit." Irenaeus also recognized the four Gospels, Acts, 13 Pauline epistles, 1 Peter, 1 John, and Revelation, as canonical Scripture (see the comments on Irenaeus).

Westcott, the nineteenth-century Anglican scholar who wrote an exhaustive book on the formation of the New Testament, says that from the time of Irenaeus, the New Testament was composed essentially of the same books as we have. He wrote, "From the close of the second century, the history of the Canon is simple, and its proof clear. It is allowed even by those who have reduced the genuine Apostolic works to the narrowest limits that from the time of Irenaeus, the New Testament was composed essentially of the same books that we receive at present and that they were regarded with the same reverence as is now shown to them" (Westcott, p. 6).

Cairns says, "The New Testament was substantially completed by A.D. 175" (Cairns, p. 118). McDonald concedes that most churches at the end of the second century agreed with the core of Irenaeus' collection of New Testament books (McDonald, p. 298).

Hans von Campenhausen, author of a scholarly work on the canon that cites an enormous amount of primary source material with voluminous footnotes, opens his concluding chapter with these words, "I have brought this history of the formation of the Christian Canon—a term which was still not used of the Bible during the period we have surveyed—to a close with Origen, and have deliberately refrained from carrying it beyond him. It is undisputed that both the Old and the New Testaments had, in essence, already reached their final form and significance around the year 200. The minor variations, which persist and are occasionally the subject of further discussion, co-exist happily with the overriding conviction that Christians everywhere possess one and the same Bible. For the fundamental understanding of the Canon, they are of no importance. If, therefore, we wish to form some picture of the motives behind the formation of the Canon and to assess its significance, then the best course is to choose a standpoint not later than the beginning of the third century and to survey the earlier development from there" (von Campenhausen, p. 327). Note carefully, this scholar stopped his work with Origen because it is "undisputed" that both Testaments "had in essence already reached their final form and significance around the year 200."

Bruce contends that from the time of Irenaeus, "the whole church in the east and west has acknowledged the New Testament collection as making up, together with the Old Testament, the Christian Bible" (Bruce, CS, p. 177). Bruce begins his book on the canon by saying that despite the attacks on the consensus view that the New Treatment was substantially fixed by the end of the second century, it continues to stand "because it is supported by weighty evidence, as shown in Bruce Metzger's magnificent work on *The Canon of the New Testament*" (Bruce, CS, p. 9).

Ropes says the date was even earlier than that. He writes, "Probably as early in the second century, the year 125, someone, in some place, or some group of persons, assembled for the use and convenience of the churches the only four gospel books describing the life and teachings of Jesus Christ which were then believed to be of great antiquity and worthy of a place in such a collection" (Ropes, p. 103).

Chapter 8

THE DEBATE ABOUT THE NEW TESTAMENT

Even though it appears the issue of the canon was basically settled by the end of the second century, there was still some debate about it. Some books in the Bible were questioned, and some that are not were thought of by some as Scripture.

Thiessen says, "Generally speaking, from the time of Irenaeus on, the New Testament contained practically the same books as we receive today and were regarded with the same reverence that we bestow on them today." He adds that there was a minority who continued to question the genuineness of some of the books for a long time (Thiessen, p. 10). Harrison contends that the consentient testimony of Irenaeus, Clement of Alexandria, and Tertullian, all close to the end of the second century, "is sufficient to establish that there was a body of authoritative writings revered by the church as a whole. The only question that remains unsettled is the extent of the canon, which involves a discussion of the disputed books" (Everett Harrison, p. 100).

The Debated Books

It should not surprise the child of God that some would doubt anything connected with God. Doubt was the original tool of Satan (Gen. 3:1). Doubt, differences of opinion, and even division are not only normal; they are also necessary. Paul explains, "For first of all, when you come together as a church, I hear that there are divisions among you, and in part I believe it. For there must also be factions among you, that those who are approved may be recognized among you" (1 Cor. 11:18-19). Differences are needed to help the discerning determine the truth.

Overview In the third and fourth centuries, some of the books of the New Testament were debated. Ryrie says, "The unqualified candidates for books to be included in the canon were rejected during this period; most of the New Testament books were received; only a few were debated" (Ryrie, p. 109).

Origen (ca. A.D. 185-254, Cairns, p. 111) recognized a New Testament collection alongside the Old Testament (Bruce, CS, p. 192). He distinguished between the *homologoumena*, the books universally recognized as Scripture, and the *antilegomena*, the books more or less opposed. In the former group, he included the four Gospels, Acts, thirteen Epistles of Paul, 1 Peter, 1 John, and Revelation; in the latter, he placed Hebrews, James, 2 Peter, 2 and 3 John, Jude, Barnabas, the Shepherd, the Didache, and the Gospel of the Hebrews (Thiessen, pp. 10-11).

He placed Hebrews in the latter category because some churches did not accept it (Bruce, CS, p. 193). Origen himself, however, frequently cited Hebrews as canonical, and cited all the other New Testament books as Scripture, except Jude, 2 and 3 John (Thiessen, p. 11). So even though Origen speaks of opposing books, He accepts all the New Testament books, except Jude, 2 and 3 John. Thiessen says Souter thinks that it is possible that Origen recognized them as genuine (Thiessen, p. 18). There is no evidence that Origen personally rejected any of the New Testament books on the opposed list.

Bruce explains that Origen "mentions all twenty-seven books of our New Testament; twenty-one, he says, are acknowledged, and six are doubtful. But among doubtful books, he also reckons some which, in the end, did not secure a place in the canon. Like Clement of Alexandria before him, he treats the *Didache* as scripture and calls the *Letter of Barnabas* a 'catholic epistle'—a term he also applies to 1 Peter. R. M. Grant suggests that while he lived in Alexandria, he accepted the more comprehensive tradition of the church there and acknowledged the *Didache* and the *Letter of Barnabas,* together with the *Shepherd* of Hermas, as scripture, but that after he moved to Caesarea and found that these books were not accepted there, he manifested greater reserve towards them. He knew 1 Clement but did not indicate if he regarded it as scripture. He had doubts about the *Preaching of Peter,* which Clement of Alexandria regarded highly. He refers to the *Gospel according to the Hebrews* and the *Acts of Paul* without at first either admitting or disputing their status as scripture; later, however, he had doubts about the *Acts of Paul"* (Bruce, CS, p. 194).

Eusebius of Caesarea (ca. A.D. 265-ca. 339, Cairns, p. 143) was the first to attempt a history of the church on a grand scale. He began his *Ecclesiastical History* in either A.D. 303 or A.D. 313. He eventually brought the story up to A.D. 324.

Like Origen, he distinguished between the *homologoumena* and the *antilegomena* but divided the latter into merely disputed and spurious ones. In other words, he had three categories: the recognized, the disputed, and the spurious. Under the recognized, he lists the four Gospels, Acts, the Epistles of Paul, 1 John, 1 Peter, and Revelation. Under those merely disputed, he mentions James, 2 Peter, 2 and 3 John, and Jude. Under those actually spurious, he lists the Acts of Paul, the Shepherd, the Apocalypse of Peter, Barnabas, the Didache, and perhaps Revelation. He lists Revelation under both the dispute and the spurious category!

Here is what Eusebius says: "At this point, it seems reasonable to summarize the writings of the New Testament which have been quoted. In the first place, the holy tetrad of the Gospels. To them follows the writing of the Acts of the Apostles. After this should be reckoned the Epistles of Paul. Following them, the Epistle of John is called the first, and, in the same way, should be recognized the Epistle of Peter. In addition to these should be put, if it seems desirable, the Revelation of John, the arguments concerning which we will expound at the proper time. These belong to the Recognized Books [homologoumenois]. Of the Disputed Books [ton d' antilegoumenon], which are nevertheless known to most, are the Epistle called of James, that of Jude, the Second Epistle of Peter, and the so-called second and third Epistles of John, which may be the work of the evangelist or of some other with the same name. Among the books which are not genuine [en tois nothois] must be reckoned the Acts of Paul, the work entitled the Shepherd, the Apocalypse of Peter, and in addition to them the letter called of

Barnabas and the so-called Teachings of the Apostles [Didache]. And in addition, as I said, the Revelation of John, if this view prevails. For, as I said, some reject it, but others count it among the Recognized Books. Some have also counted the Gospel according to the Hebrews, in which those of the Hebrews who have accepted Christ take a special pleasure. These would all belong to the disputed books, but we have nevertheless been obliged to make a list of them, distinguishing between those writings which, according to the tradition of the Church [lit., ecclesiastical tradition], are true, genuine, and recognized [scriptures] [aletheis kai aplastous kai anomologemenas graphas], and those which differ from them in that they are not canonical [ouk endiathekous] but disputed, yet nevertheless are own to most of the writers of the Church, in order that we might know them and the writings which are put forward by heretics under the name of the apostles containing gospels such as those of Peter, and Thomas, and Matthias, and some others besides, or Acts such as those of Andrew and John and the other apostles. To none of these has any who belonged to the succession of the orthodox ever thought it right to refer in his writings. Moreover, the type of phraseology differs from apostolic style, and the opinion and tendency of their contents are widely dissonant from true orthodoxy and clearly show that they are the forgeries of heretics. They ought, therefore, to be reckoned not even among spurious [en notboisl books but shunned as altogether wicked and impious" (Eusebius, *Hist. eccl.* 3.25.1-7).

Observations First, to sum up: during the third and fourth centuries, some doubted Hebrews, James, 2 Peter, 2 and 3 John, Jude, and Revelation. Origen reports that some doubted some books, but he himself accepts all the books of the New Testament, except 2 and 3 John and Jude and some scholars think it is possible that Origen recognized them as genuine. There is no evidence that Origen personally rejected any of the New Testament books on the opposed list. Eusebius lists James, 2 Peter, 2 and 3 John, and Jude as disputed, not spurious. For some reason, Eusebius fails to mention the book of Hebrews and he puts Revelation in both the dispute and the spurious category. *Thus, in some quarters, there was some questions about seven books: Hebrews, James, 2 Peter, 2 and 3 John, Jude, and the Revelation.* These books lacked "universal endorsement" (Everett Harrison, p. 101).

Second, there were different reasons why these "doubted books" were questioned.

Hebrews was questioned because of its authorship (Everett Harrison, p. 345). There is, however, early and abundant evidence for it. For example, Clement of Rome (A.D. 95) quotes it copiously and cites several first-century authors (Thiessen, pp. 297-298).

James was perhaps questioned because it was written to Jewish believers and contained little that would appeal to the "speculative mind of Greek Christians" (Tenney, p. 427). The Muratorian Fragment omitted it. Eusebius classified it as disputed but quoted it as Scripture (Eusebius, *Commentary on the Psalms*). Mayor quotes early authors beginning with Clement of Rome and concludes that James "was more widely known doing the first three centuries than has been commonly supposed" (Mayor, pp. lii-lxviii).

In his preface to the New Testament, Luther said that James is "a perfect straw epistle," compared to the Gospel of John, 1 John, the epistles of Paul, especially Romans, Galatians, Ephesians, and Peter's epistles. He complained that James did not include the gospel. Luther placed Hebrews, James, Jude, and Revelation in his German New Testament at the end, assigning them no numbers in the table of contents. Harrison says Luther distrusted James and was disappointed in it (Everett Harrison, p. 360). Ryrie observes, "Sometimes it is claimed that Martin Luther rejected the Book of James as being canonical. This is not so. Here's what he wrote in his preface to the New Testament, in which he ascribes different degrees of doctrinal value to the several books of the New Testament. 'St. John's Gospel and his first Epistle, St. Paul's Epistles, especially those to the Romans, Galatians, Ephesians, and St. Peter's Epistle—these are the books which show to thee Christ and teach everything necessary and blessed for thee to know, even if you were never to see or hear any other book of doctrine. Therefore, St. James' Epistle is a perfect straw-epistle compared with them, for it has in it nothing of an evangelic kind." Thus Luther was comparing (in his opinion) doctrinal value, not canonical validity" (Ryrie, p. 109). The Lutheran Church has not followed Luther's evaluation of James.

Second Peter was questioned because of its difference in style from 1 Peter. Jerome says some hesitation in accepting 2 Peter was because it was so different from 1 Peter (Jerome, *Epistle to*

Hedibia, 120; see also Tenney, p. 427). Even Calvin was unsure of 2 Peter (Tenney, p. 428)! Lumby says, "It is almost inconceivable that a forger, writing to warn against false teachers, writing in the interest of truth, should have thus deliberately assumed a name and experience to which he had no claim" (Thiessen, p. 288). Could it be that some reject this letter because it rejects them?

Second John was questioned perhaps because there were few early quotations or definite allusions to it. Irenaeus attributes 2 John 11 to John, the disciple of the Lord (Irenaeus, *Against Heresies*, I. xvi. 3) and assigns 2 John 7-8 to the Apostle John (Irenaeus, *Against Heresies*, III. xvi. 8). Origen says some doubted it, but he does not seem to reject it (Everett Harrison, p. 422).

Third John was questioned probably for the same reason as 2 John. The evidence for it is less than for 2 John, but as has been mentioned, Goodspeed claims that the early writers included 2 and 3 John with 1 John, which is what Irenaeus did (See Thiessen, p. 22).

Jude was questioned because for several reasons. Eusebius lists it as a disputed book but in another place, calls it spurious because not many ancients made use of it (Eusebius, *Hist. eccl.* II. xxiii. 25). Jerome says some rejected it because of its supposed reference to the book of Enoch (Jerome, *Lives of Illustrious Men*, ch. 4). On the other hand, Tertullian considered Enoch Scripture, because of Jude's use of it!

Thiessen explains: "Clement of Alexandria, Tertullian, Jerome, Augustine, and the Church Fathers generally held that Jude quotes from several apocryphal books. It was on this ground that they long rejected it. It was held that at vs. 9 the writer quotes from the Assumption of Moses and at vs. 14 f. from the Book of Enoch. Philippi vigorously denied this, saying that Jude merely wrote from oral tradition, and this is possible. The fragment of the Assumption of Moses that has come down to us is broken off before the burial of Moses is reached, and we really cannot tell what followed in the part that is missing. There is a great similarity between Enoch 1:9; 5:4 and Jude 14 f. Moorehead admits the possibility of a quotation in both instances. With regard to the Book of Enoch in particular, he says: 'Granting such quotation, that fact does not warrant us to affirm that he endorses the book. Paul cites from three Greek poets: from Aratus (Acts 17:28), from Menander, and from Epimenides the apostle adds, 'This testimony is true' (Tit. 1:13), but no one imagines he means to say the whole poem is true' (Tit. 1:13), but no one imagines he means to say the whole poem is true. So Jude cites a passage from a non-canonical book not because he accepts the whole book as true, but this particular prediction he receives as from God.' This seems to us to be a satisfactory solution to the problem" (Thiessen, pp. 294-295).

Revelation was not questioned at first. Harrison points out, "John's Apocalypse had a solid place in the canon in the earlier patristic period, being questioned only by the sect known as the Alogi, but generally received throughout the church. The failure of writers in the East during the fourth century to include it in the New Testament may be assigned to the influence of the criticism of Dionysius of Alexandria, who argued the great differences between the Revelation and the Fourth Gospel as ground for concluding that another John must have written the Apocalypse. Influenced by Dionysius, Eusebius felt that it was wise to put the book not only among the acknowledged writings (Homologoumena) but also with the non-genuine, saying that some reject it" (Everett Harrison, p. 101).

Baker says, "By the end of the fourth century, the doubts associated with these seven books were removed and all were accepted as canonical" (Baker, p. 85).

The Rejected Books

It should not surprise the child of God that some would attempt to imitate the Word of God. "Satan himself transforms himself into an angel of light" (2 Cor. 11:14). Even in Paul's day, false teachers circulated letters purportedly written by him (2 Thess. 2:2).

Spurious Books In the early centuries of church history, some books were accepted as canonical that are not in the Protestant New Testament. According to Baker, "The New Testament Apocrypha consists of gospels and epistles written under the name of an apostle or a well-known leader. Some fifteen of these extra-canonical books have been listed: The Teaching of the Twelve Apostles (the *Didache*), The Epistle of Barnabas, The First Epistle of Clement, the Second Epistle of Clement, The Shepard of Hermas, The Apocalypse of Peter, The Acts of Paul, including Paul and Thecla, The Epistle of Polycarp to the Philippians, The Seven Epistles of Ignatius, The Gospel of Pseudo-Matthew, The Protevangelium of James, The Gospel of the Nativity of Mary,

The Gospel of Nicodemus, The Gospel of the Savior's Infancy, and the History of Joseph the Carpenter" (Baker, pp. 85-86).

Harrison suggests that some books were considered canonical by some Christians because they were thought to be apostolic. He points to the fact that the full name of the *Didache* is the Teaching of the Twelve Apostles. Clement of Rome was thought to be the Clement mentioned in Philippians 4:3 (Clement of Alexander, Origen). The acceptance of the *Shepherd of Hermas* in some quarters is traced to the belief that the author was the one mentioned in Romans 16:14 (Everett Harrison, pp. 104-105).

Eusebius explains, "Some have also counted [as canonical or recognized] the Gospel according to the Hebrews in which those of the Hebrews who have accepted Christ take a special pleasure. These would all belong to the disputed books, but we have nevertheless been obliged to make a list of them, distinguishing between those writings which, according to the tradition of the Church, are true, genuine, and recognized and those which differ from them in that they are not canonical but disputed, yet nevertheless are known to most of the writers of the Church, in order that we might know them and the writings which are put forward by heretics under the name of the apostles containing gospels such as those of Peter, and Thomas, and Matthias, and some others besides, or Acts such as those of Andrew and John and the other apostles. To none of these has any who belonged to the succession of the orthodox ever thought it right to refer in his writings. Moreover, the type and phraseology differs from apostolic style, and the opinion and tendency of their contents is widely dissonant from true orthodoxy and clearly shows that they are the forgeries of heretics. They ought, therefore, to be reckoned not even among spurious books but shunned as altogether wicked and impious" (Eusebius, *Hist. Eccl.* 3.25:6-7).

The Shepherd of Hermas (ca. A.D. 150) Irenaeus regarded *The Shepherd of Hermas* as Scripture; Clement of Alexandria said that it made its statements "divinely" and although Origen seems to express doubts about it, he recognized it as divinely inspired. Sinaiticus (fourth century) lists Hermas with the canonical books of the New Testament (Kistemaker, p. 7).

The Muratorian Fragment (A.D. 170) says, "the *Shepherd* was written *by* Hermas in the city *of* Rome quite recently, in our own times, when his brother Pius occupied the bishop's chair in the church *of* the city *of* Rome; and therefore it may be read indeed, but cannot be given out to the people in church either among the prophets, since their number is complete, *or* among the apostles at the end *of* the times" (cited by Bruce, CS, p. 161).

Before Tertullian (A.D. 160-225) became a Montanist, he included the Shepherd of Hermas in his collection of Scripture*s*, but he later dismissed it "with scorn" (McDonald, p. 304). In his treatise on modesty (chap. 10), he states that the *Shepherd of Hermas* had been "habitually judged by every council of churches … among apocryphal and false (writings)."

The point is that there were spurious books claiming to be from the apostles, and some Christians did accept a few of them, but the early Church was aware of this problem and rejected those books that were not inspired.

The Debate About The New Testament

The Saying of Jesus According to the Apostle John, besides what is recorded in his gospel, "many other things that Jesus did, which if they were written one by one, I suppose that even the world itself could not contain the books that would be written" (Jn. 21:25). Surely, not all of the *sayings* of Jesus are recorded in the four Gospels of the New Testament.

Sure enough, there are sayings of Jesus that have been recorded outside the New Testament. In fact, there are 266 supposed sayings of Jesus not found in the canonical Gospels (called *agrapha*). The problem is determining if any of these are authentic and, if so, which ones. Jeremias has said that only eighteen are authentic (McDonald, p. 8 fn. 8., 282). Even if we could determine that one or more of the sayings were genuine, evidently, God did not intend that they be part of His inspired Word; that alone is sufficient to bring believers to spiritual maturity and equip them for every good work (2 Tim. 3:16-17). In other words, even a genuine saying of Jesus recorded outside the Bible is not part of God's Word.

The Gospel of the Infancy of Jesus Christ The *Gospel of the Infancy of Jesus Christ* contains the story of some sisters whose brother was bewitched by a woman and turned into a mule. The sisters came to the Virgin Mary for help: "Hereupon St. Mary was grieved at their case, and taking the Lord Jesus, put him upon the back of the mule. And said to her son, O Jesus Christ, restore according to thy extraordinary power this mule, and grant him to have again the shape of a man and a rational creature, as he had formerly. This was scarce said by the Lady St. Mary, but the mule immediately passed into a human form, and became a young man without any deformity" (*The Gospel of the Infancy of Jesus Christ* 7:24-26).

The Epistle of Barnabas In discussing the dietary laws of Leviticus, *The Epistle of Barnabas* says, "Neither shalt thou eat of the hyena; that is, again, be not an adulterer, nor a corruptor of others; neither be like to such. And wherefore so?-because that creature every year changes its kind, and is sometimes male and sometimes female" (*The Epistle of Barnabas* 9:8).

The Gospel of Thomas According to *The Gospel of Thomas*, "Another time Jesus went forth into the street, and a boy running by, rushed upon his shoulder; at which Jesus being angry, said to him, thou shalt go no farther. And he instantly fell down dead" (*The Gospel of Thomas* 2:7-9). *The Gospel of Thomas* concludes with these words, "Simon Peter said to them, 'Mary, leave us, for women are not worthy of life.' Jesus said, 'I myself shall lead her in order to make her male, so that she too may become a living spirit resembling you males. For every woman who will make herself male will enter the kingdom of heaven" (*The Gospel of Thomas*, 114).

Bruce makes the interesting observation, "It is remarkable, when one comes to think of it, that the four canonical Gospels are anonymous, whereas the 'Gospels' which proliferated in the late second century and afterward claimed to have been written by apostles and other eyewitnesses. Catholic churchmen found it necessary, therefore, to defend the apostolic authenticity of the Gospels, which they accepted against the claims of those which they rejected. Hence come the accounts of the origin of the canonical four which appear in the Muratorian list, in the so-called anti-Marcionite prologues, and in Irenaeus" (Bruce, CS, p. 257).

The Jesus Seminar The Jesus Seminar is a group of critical scholars who vote to decide the historicity of the deeds and sayings of Jesus. This group would like to reduce the biblical canon by eliminating apocalyptic literature such as, Matthew 24 and Mark 13, as well as the book of Revelation. It would also like to expand the biblical canon to include the Gospel of Thomas and the "Unknown Gospel" (MacDonald, p. 10).

Summary: In the third and fourth centuries, some canonical books were doubted and some books were rejected.

It should be noted that thirty-four books in the Old Testament and twenty in the New Testament have little or no dispute (Baker, p. 84).

"Passing disagreement on a few books should not be allowed to overshadow in importance a greater measure of agreement on the majority of the books. Furthermore, basic agreement on the canon by various sections of the church on a voluntary basis (apart from and prior to action by church councils) is a noteworthy fact that should be given its full weight" (Everett Harrison, p. 113).

Are there lost books of the Bible? Ryrie says, "Even if a letter of Paul were discovered, it would not be canonical. After all, Paul must have written many letters during his lifetime in addition to the ones that are in the New Testament, yet the church did not include them in the canon. Not everything an apostle wrote was inspired, for it was not the writer who was inspired but his writings, and not necessarily all of them" (Ryrie, p. 106).

Chapter 9

FORMAL RECOGNITION OF THE NEW TESTAMENT

Eventually, there was a formal recognition of the Protestant New Testament, but that was merely a formal *recognition*, not a *formation* of the New Testament. For example, McDonald points out, "When the term *canon* came to mean a fairly precise collection of sacred writings in the latter part of the fourth century C.E., the canonical Gospels were already in the place of priority in all such collections and were often placed in the same order that they are found in the Bible today" (McDonald, p. 290). Here is a brief survey of the recognition of a specific canon in extant writings.

Early Recognition

Before considering the formal recognition of the canon, *Origen* (A.D. 185-254) speaks of the "canonized Scriptures" (commentary on Mt., sec. 28). He speaks of our Gospels "which alone are uncontroverted in the church of God spread under heaven" and names them" (Eusebius, *Hist. Eccl.* VI. xxv. 4). In his commentary on Joshua, he says that Paul thundered with the fourteen "trumpets" of his epistles. He also indicates some doubt in the church of his time about 2 Peter and 2 and 3 John. "Little, if anything, of the complete New Testament is lacking in Origen and therefore in the Egyptian church of his time" (Everett Harrison, p. 100).

Eusebius (A.D. 265-339) As pointed out, Eusebius listed the four Gospels, Acts, the Epistles of Paul, 1 John, 1 Peter, and Revelation as recognized books. He listed only James, 2 Peter, 2 and 3 John, Jude, and Revelation as disputed books (Everett Harrison, p. 102).

Council of Nicaea (A.D. 325) did not discuss the canon question, but Arius and Athanasius's followers used Scripture for their arguments.

Cyril (A.D. 315-386; McDonald, p. 381) Cyril, Bishop of Jerusalem (315-386), accepted all but Revelation (Everett Harrison, p. 102).

Formal Recognition

Athanasius (A.D. 367). The council of Nicaea (325) settled the issue of when to commemorate Easter. From A.D. 328 to A.D. 373, Athanasius, Bishop of Alexandria, wrote an annual letter to his churches announcing the date for Easter. In his 39th letter (A.D. 367), he identified the canon of the Old and New Testaments. He is probably the first to use the term "canon" about a close collection of sacred literature (McDonald, p. 380). For the New Testament, he listed all 27 books (Harrison, p. 102). He included the books of the Old Testament but excluded the Apocrypha (Sheeley, p. 519).

Formal Recognition of The New Testament

Council of Laodicea (A.D. 363) was a local gathering chiefly from the region of Phrygia (Tenney, p. 426). It was attended by only a few delegates (Everett Harrison, p. 103). The 59th canon decreed that only canonical books of the New Testament could be read in the churches (Tenney, p. 426). All the books of the New Testament were listed except Revelation. However, since not all the sources have this final canon of the council, the list of books was probably added later (Everett Harrison, p. 103).

The Third Council of Carthage (A.D. 397) is the first council to formally decide on a canon. They declared that the 27 books of the New Treatment were to be received as canonical, and only those books were to be received.

Council of Hippo (A.D. 419) repeated the same list of canonical books as the Council of Carthage.

Summary: After general recognition of books of the New Testament as Scripture and even recognition of a canon, there was finally a formal recognition of the twenty-seven book New Treatment.

These men and councils did not formulate the canon or choose the books to form the Bible. They merely formally *recognized* the choice already made among the churches. They merely stated publicly what the churches had accepted for some time. Actually, the churches did not determine what books should be in the Bible either; God did. "The books were inspired when they were written and, thus, canonical. The church only attested to what was inherently true" (Ryrie, p. 108).

The popular impression is that church councils determined the canon. Harrison states, "It has sometimes been asserted that the canon derives both its form and authority from church councils, as though the church had no recognized Scripture prior to their action. Such is not the case. What the councils did was to certify the canon that was already widely acknowledged in the church." Harrison goes on to say that the church councils "did not provide for the first time a rule of faith and practice but rather gave public and united testimony to that which the church had long known and used and cherished as its authoritative guide." He adds that even in the case of disputed books councils were only "speaking in behalf of the majority who already received these books as Scripture" (Harrison, p. 103).

Chapter 10

CONCLUSION

How was the Bible formed? Who determined which books were included and which books were excluded? What standard was used to make such determinations? What conclusions can be drawn after looking at the available data from both inside and outside the Bible?

All agree that there is no record inside or outside of the Bible of the formation of the Bible. There is no surviving report of anyone saying that, at this point, the canon was closed.

The Scriptures

From the Scriptures themselves, it is apparent that in the case of the Law (the five books of Moses), the Prophets (the rest of the Old Testament), the Gospels (four books), and the epistles (the remainder of the New Testament), God spoke, men wrote what God spoke or what He moved them to write, and God influenced people so that they took note that what was written was the Word of God. It is also obvious that many other books were written during the Old Testament period. By the time Luke wrote, *many other gospels* had been written (Lk. 1:1-4), and during the lifetime of the Apostle Paul, *letters were written* in his name (2 Thess. 2:2). Therefore, there was a selection process.

Based on what Jesus said about the Scripture and the doctrine of inspiration, it is logical to assume that God inspired His Word for people beyond the original recipients. He providentially worked to see to it that His Word was recognized. Inspiration and canonization are the work of God. He is the One who determined which books were included and which books were excluded. That is the traditional evangelical view.

The canon does not derive its authority from the sanction of Jewish priests and leaders or the Christian Church. That authority is in itself. The collection of the canon is merely the assembling into one volume of those books whose sacred character and claim have already secured general acknowledgment (Unger, pp. 73-74).

At the end of his book on the canon, Bruce says, "The theological aspect of canonization has not been the subject of this book, which has been concerned rather with the historical aspect, but for those who receive the scriptures as God's Word written the theological aspect is the most important" (Bruce, CS, p. 281). He adds, "The work of the Holy Spirit is not discerned by means of the common tools of the historian's trade. His inner witness gives the assurance to hearers or readers of scripture that, in its words, God himself is addressing them, but when one is considering the process by which the canon of scripture took shape, it would be wiser to speak of the providence or guidance of the Spirit than of his witness" (Bruce, CS, p. 281).

William Barclay says, "The New Testament books became canonical because no one could stop them doing so," and Cullmann says, "The books which were to form the future canon *forced themselves on the Church by their intrinsic apostolic authority,* as they do still because the *Kyrios* Christ speaks in them" (Cullmann, cited by Bruce, CS, p. 282).

Ancient Authors

Ancient authors were aware of the inspiration of the Scripture. Clement of Rome said Paul wrote to the Corinthians "under the inspiration of the Spirit" (1 Clement 47:1-3). Irenaeus makes it clear that the Scriptures, even when they are not clearly understood, "were spoken by the Word of God and by His Spirit" (Irenaeus, *Haer.* 2.28.2). Theophilus of Antioch (ca. 180) asserts, "The holy writings teach us, and all the spirit-bearing ... that at first God was alone, and Word in Him" (Theophilus, *Autol.* 2.22). Inspiration involved "men of God carrying in them a holy spirit and becoming prophets, being inspired and made wise by God, became God-taught, and holy and righteous" (Theophilus, *Autol.* 2:9). Origen maintained that "the Scriptures were written by the Spirit of God" (Irenaeus, *First Principles* preface 8). Seeking to discredit the Doctrine of Peter, he says that he can show that it was not written by Peter "or by any other person inspired by the Spirit of God" (*First Principles* preface 8). The operating assumption here, of course, is that Scripture is inspired, but heresy and falsehood are not.

The "Festal Letter" of Athanasius (A.D. 367) distinguishes sharply between "God-inspired Scripture ... handed down to our fathers by those who were eyewitnesses and servants of the word from the beginning" and the "so-called secret writings" of heretics. Athanasius' list comprised the four Gospels, Acts, James, I and II Peter, I, II, and III John, Jude, Romans, I and II Corinthians, Galatians, Ephesians, Philippians, Colossians, I and II Thessalonians, Hebrews, I and II Timothy, Titus, Philemon, Revelation. "These," said Athanasius, "are springs of salvation ... let no one add to them or take away from them."

Modern Scholars

Modern scholars have acknowledged that the issue in canonization is inspiration. Westcott "emphasized the importance of a superintending providence guiding the church from the beginning to an appreciation of the books that time and use confirmed" (Everett Harrison, p. 107). Concerning the canon, Westcott writes, "Its limits were fixed in the earliest times by use rather than by criticism; and this use itself was based on immediate knowledge" (Westcott, p. 496). Again, he affirms that it was under the influence of the Spirit that the church recognized in the New Testament the law of its constitution (Westcott, p. 498). The formation of the canon was an act of the intuition of the church (Westcott, p. 498).

Karl Barth states, "In no sense of the concept could or can the Church give the Canon to itself. The Church cannot 'form' it, as historians have occasionally said, without being aware of the theological implications. The Church can only confirm or establish it as something which has already been formed and given" (Karl Barth, *Church Dogmatics*, I/2, p. 473).

As Tenney concludes, canonicity cannot be determined by authorship nor by the church's acceptance. "The church did not *determine* the canon; it *recognized* the canon" (Tenney, p. 421). "The true criterion of canonicity is inspiration" (Tenney, p. 418). As Tenney explains, if inspiration is the essential quality of canonicity, no council could create a canon because no group could not inspire what was already inspired! All any council could do is give their opinion concerning which books were canonical and let history justify or reverse their verdict (Tenney, p. 421).

Summary: Inspiration determines canonicity. God inspired His Word and saw to it that it was recognized as His Word.

Here is a succinct summary. The Bible claims to be the Word of God (2 Tim. 3:16). Beginning with Moses, God spoke to men who wrote what God said to them or God moved them to write (2 Pet. 1:21). Both the Old Testament and the New Testament record there was an immediate recognition that what was written was the Word of God (Dan. 9:2; 1 Tim. 5:18; 2 Pet 3:15-16).

In the case of the Old Testament, there are indications outside the Bible that the prophets ceased after the last Old Testament book was written (Josephus, etc.). The New Testament, in general, and Jesus, in particular, speak of the Old Testament as if there was a closed canon (see "the Law and the Prophets" in Lk. 11:50-51, 24:44).

In the case of the New Testament, what can be said about information outside the Bible is as follows:

1. Immediately after the last book of the New Testament was written (A.D. 95), books of the New Testament were known and used as authority, and some were called inspired (1 Clement does that).

2. During the second century, the books of the New Testament were recognized as Scripture, and there are indications that there was a canon. There is no list of all the books in the New Testament, but by the end of the second century, there is evidence that the four Gospels, Acts, the epistles of Paul, 1 Peter, 1 John, and Revelation, were recognized as canonical Scripture (Irenaeus). Most churches at the end of the second century were in basic agreement with the core of Irenaeus' collection of New Testament books (McDonald, p. 298). In fact, Westcott says, "From the time of Irenaeus, the New Testament was composed essentially of the same books which we receive at present, and that they were regarded with the same reverence as is now shown to them" (Westcott, p. 6).

3. In the third and fourth centuries, some doubted some of the books in the New Testament, and during this time, some of the non-canonical books were declared spurious (see statements by Origen and Eusebius).

4. In the fourth century, there was formal recognition of what the church had already recognized.

As a deist, Thomas Jefferson embraced the notion of a well-ordered universe created by a God who withdrew into detached

Conclusion

transcendence and rejected the miraculous and prophetic elements in the Bible. Jefferson once promised a friend, Philadelphia physician Benjamin Rush, that he would summarize his views on Christianity. "In a letter to Rush on April 21, 1803, Jefferson said his editing experiment aimed to see whether the ethical teachings of Jesus could be separated from elements he believed were attached to Christianity over the centuries. 'To the corruption of Christianity I am indeed opposed,' he wrote to Rush, 'but not to the genuine precepts of Jesus himself.'"

So, as Sahagum explains, "Thomas Jefferson set to work with scissors, snipping out every miracle and inconsistency he could find in the New Testament Gospels of Matthew, Mark, Luke, and John. Then, relying on a cut-and-paste technique, he reassembled the excerpts into what he believed was a more coherent narrative and pasted them onto blank paper—alongside translations in French, Greek, and Latin. In a letter sent from Monticello to John Adams in 1813, Jefferson said his 'wee little book' of 46 pages was based on a lifetime of inquiry and reflection and contained 'the most sublime and benevolent code of morals which has ever been offered to man. He called the book 'The Life and Morals of Jesus of Nazareth.' Friends dubbed it the Jefferson Bible.'"

Sahagum adds, "'I have performed the operation for my own use,' he (Jefferson) continued, 'by cutting verse by verse out of the printed book, and arranging the matter, which is evidently his and which is as easily distinguished as diamonds in a dunghill.'"

"In Jefferson's version of the Gospels, for example, Jesus is still wrapped in swaddling clothes after his birth in Bethlehem.

But no angel tells shepherds watching their flocks by night that a Savior has been born. Jefferson retains Jesus' crucifixion but ends the text with his burial, not with the resurrection. Stripping miracles from the story of Jesus was among the ambitious projects of a man with a famously restless mind. At 71, he read Plato's 'Republic' in the original Greek and found it lackluster."

Robert C. Ritchie, director of research at the Huntington Library, said, "For a lot of people, taking scissors to the Bible would be such an act of desecration they wouldn't do it, yet it gives a reading into Jefferson's take on the Bible, which was not as divine word put into print, but as a book that can be cut up." Ritchie also said, "For Jefferson, the Bible was a book that could be made and unmade."

"Jefferson was a particular fan of Joseph Priestley, a scientist, ordained minister and one of Jefferson's friends. Priestley—who discovered oxygen and invented carbonated water and the rubber eraser—published books that infamously cast a critical eye upon biblical miracles."

"Say nothing of my religion," Jefferson once said. "It is known to myself and my God alone. Its evidence before the world is to be sought in my life; if that has been honest and dutiful to society, the religion which has regulated it cannot be a bad one."

(Edited from Louis Sahagun, "A Founding Father's View of God," *Los Angeles Times*, July 5, 2008. A Facsimile of the Jefferson Bible is at the Huntington Library and an online version can be seen at www.monticello.org/library/links/jefferson.html.)

Regarding the formation of the Bible, we can either believe

Conclusion

Jesus or Jefferson. Jesus says, "The Scripture cannot be broken" (Jn. 10:35). Jefferson says cut up the Scripture and you decide what is the Word of God. I choose to follow Jesus.

APPENDIX

EARLY REFERENCES TO THE NEW TESTAMENT

Shortly after the completion of the New Testament (A.D. 95), ancient authors quoted or alluded to it. These references indicate that these books existed and, in many cases, that the New Testament books were considered authoritative and even inspired. Clement (A.D. 95) reminds the Corinthians that "the blessed apostle Paul" wrote to them "under the inspiration of the spirit" (1 Clement, Chapter 47). So, after the New Testament was written, it was considered inspired (1 Tim. 5:18; 2 Pet. 15-16, Clement).

NT Book	NT Reference	Ancient Author	Reference
Mat.	6:25 7:1	Diognetus (A.D. 100) Polycarp (A.D. 110)	Ch. 9 Ch. 2
Mark	9:42, 14:21	Clement (A.D. 95)	Ch. 46
Luke	10:7	Paul (A.D. 63)	1 Tim. 5:18
John	17:11, 14, 16	Diognetus (A.D. 100)	Ch. 6
Acts	20:35	Clement (A.D. 95)	Ch. 2
Ro.	9:5/1:32 14:10-12	Clement (A.D. 95) Polycarp (A.D. 110)	Ch. 31/35 Ch. 6
1 Cor.	Paul wrote under inspiration	Clement (A.D. 95)	Ch. 47
2 Cor.	10:3, 6:10	Diognetus (A.D. 100)	Ch. 5
Gal.	2:9 4:10	Clement (A.D. 95) Diognetus (A.D. 100)	Ch. 5 Ch. 4

Appendix

NT Book	NT Reference	Ancient Author	Reference
Ephesians	4:4-6	Clement (A.D. 95)	Ch. 46
Philippians	3:20	Study Paul's letter to you Diognetus (A.D. 100) Polycarp (A.D. 110)	Ch. 5 Ch. 3
Colossians	1:18	Clement (A.D. 95)	Ch. 24
1 Thess.	5:17/5:22	Polycarp (A.D. 110)	Ch. 4/11
2 Thess.	3:15	Polycarp (A.D. 110)	Ch. 11
1 Timothy	3:166;7,10	Diognetus (A.D. 100) Polycarp (A.D. 110)	Ch. 11 Ch. 4
2 Timothy	1:32:12	Clement (A.D. 95) Polycarp (A.D. 110)	Ch. 45 Ch.5
Titus	3:1/2:10	Clement (A.D. 95)	Ch. 2/26
Philemon	20	Ignatius (A.D. 116)	Eph. I
Hebrews	1:2, 3, 4, 6, 13/3:5/11:37	Clement (A.D. 95) James 3:13 Clement (A.D. 95)	Ch. 36/43/17 Ch. 38
1 Peter	1:19/4:8	Clement (A.D. 95)	Ch. 7/49
2 Peter	3:15	Polycarp (A.D. 110)	Ch. 3
1 John	4:2-3	Polycarp (A.D. 110)	Ch. 7
2 John	May be incl. with 1 Jn.	Irenaeus	
3 John	May be incl. with 1 Jn.	Irenaeus	
Jude	3/20	Polycarp (A.D. 110)	Ch. 3
Revelation	22:12	Clement (A.D. 95)	Ch. 34

BIBLIOGRAPHY

Gleason, Archer. *A Survey of the Old Testament.* Grand Rapids: Wm. B. Eerdmans, 1962.

Baker, Charles F. *A Dispensational Theology.* Grand Rapids: Grace Bible College Publications, 1971.

Beckwith, R. T. *Old Testament Canon of the New Testament Church and its Background in Early Judaism.* Grand Rapids: Eerdmans, 1985.

Bruce, F. F. *The Canon of Scripture.* Downer Grove, IL: Intervarsity Press, 1988.

Bush, George. *Notes on Joshua.* New York: Newman & Ivison. 1852. Reprinted by James and Klock Publishing of Minneapolis in 1976.

Cairns, Earle E. *Christianity Through the Century.* Grand Rapids: Zondervan, 1981.

Campenhausen, Hans von. *The Formation of the Christian Bible.* Translated by J. A. Baker. Mifflintown, PA: Sigler Press, 1977.

Campbell, Donald K. *No Time for Neutrality.* Wheaton: Victor Books, 1981.

Chafer, Lewis Sperry, *Systematic Theology.* Dallas: Dallas Seminary Press, 1947.

Ewert, David. *From Ancient Tablets to Modern Translations: A General Introduction to the Bible.* Grand Rapids: Zondervan, 1983.

Farnell, David F. "The Synoptic Gospels in the Ancient Church: A Testimony to the Priority of Matthew's Gospel." The Master's Seminary Journal, 10:1 (1999).

Geisler, Norman L. Christian Apologetics. Peabody, MA: Prince Press, 2002.

Harrison, Roland Kenneth. Introduction to the Old Testament. Grand Rapids: Wm. B. Eerdmans, 1969.

Harrison, Everett F. Introduction to the New Testament. Grand Rapids: Wm. B. Eerdmans, 1968.

Hiebert, D. Edmond. An Introduction to the Non-Pauline Epistle. Chicago: Moody Press, 1969.

Hill, C. E. "The Debate over the Muratorian Fragment and the Development of the Canon," Westminster Theological Journal, 57:2, Fall 199, pp. 437-452.

Kistemaker, Simon J. "The Canon of the New Testament." Journal of the Evangelical Theological Society, 20/1, Winter, 1977.

Keil C. F., and Delitzsch F. Biblical Commentary on the Books of Samuel. Grand Rapids: Wm. B. Eerdmans, 1962.

Laetsch, Theo. Jeremiah. Saint Louis: Concordia Publishing House, 1965.

Mayor, Joseph B., The Epistle of St. James. London: Macmillan and Co., 1897.

McDonald, Lee Martin, The Biblical Canon. Peabody, MA: Hendrickson, 2008.

Miller, H. S., *General Biblical Introduction*. Houghton, NY: The Word Bearer Press, 1947.

Nicole, Roger. "The Canon of the New Testament," *Journal of the Evangelical Theological Society*, vol. 40 June 1997, pp. 199-206.

Ridderbos, Herman. *The Authority of the New Testament Scriptures*. Philadelphia: Presbyterian & Reformed Publishing Co., 1963.

Ryrie, Charles C. *Basic Theology*. Wheaton, Illinois: Victor Books, 1986.

Sawyer, M. James. "Evangelicals and the Canon of the New Testament," *Grace Theological Journal*, vol. 11, #1, Spring 1990, pp. 29-52.

Sheeley, Steven M. "From 'Scripture' to 'Canon': the Development of the New Testament Canon," *Review and Expositor*, vol. 95:4, Fall 1998.

Tenney, Merrill C. *The New Testament: An Historical and Analytic Survey*. Grand Rapids: Wm. B. Eerdmans, 1960.

Thiessen, Henry C. *Introduction to the New Testament*. Grand Rapids: Wm. B. Eerdmans, 1962.

Thompson, J. A. *The Book of Jeremiah*, The New International Commentary on the Old Testament, Grand Rapids: Wm. B. Eerdmans, 1987.

Unger, Merrill F. *Introductory Guide to the Old Testament*. Grand Rapids: Zondervan Publishing House, 1956.

Warfield, B. B. *The Inspiration and Authority of the Bible*, Grand Rapids: Baker Book House, 1981.

Westcott, B. F. *A General Survey of the History of the Canon of the New Testament.* London: MacMillan, 1855; 6th edition 1889; reprinted, Grand Rapids, 1980.

Woudstra M. H. *The Book of Joshua*, The New International Commentary on the Old Testament, Grand Rapids: Wm. B. Eerdmans, 1985.

Yarborough, Robert W. "The Date of Papias: A Reassessment," *Journal of the Evangelical Theological Society*, vol. 26, pp. 181-82.

Young, E. J. "The Canon of the Old Testament," *Revelation and the Bible*, p. 168.

About The Author

G. Michael Cocoris is a gifted communicator. He can make even complicated subjects simple, clear, and practical. His breadth of experience has allowed him to relate to a wide range of audiences.

Michael received a Bachelor of Arts degree from Tennessee Temple University, a Master of Theology degree from Dallas Seminary, and a Doctorate of Divinity from Biola University. He traveled the United States for over a dozen years as a speaker. He has also been a seminary professor, visiting lecturer, and world traveler, including hosting tours to Israel and China.

Michael has pastored three churches, including a rural church when he was in seminary, an urban church, the historic Church of the Open Door, first in downtown Los Angeles and later in Glendora, California, and a suburban church, the Lindley Church in Tarzana California, a suburb of Los Angeles. While at the Church of Open Door, he had a daily radio broadcast.

Michael has written numerous magazine articles, mainly for *Biblical Research Monthly*. He has authored a number of books, including *Seventy Years on Hope Street, A History of the Church of the Open Door*; *The Spiritual Life, Clarifying the Confusion; Repentance, The Most Misunderstood Word in the Bible; Evangelism: A Biblical Approach; The Salvation Controversy; Lordship Salvation: Is It Biblical?; The Books of the Bible, the Subject, Structure, Situation, and Significant Verses of Each Book; Psalms, A Song for Every Situation, Each Summarized on One Page; and Counseling Theories: A Simple Explanation and Biblical Evaluation*. In addition, he was a contributor to The *NKJV Study Bible* and *Nelson's New Illustrated Bible Commentary*.

Michael is the pastor of the Lindley Church in Tarzana, California. He and his wife, Patricia, live in Santa Monica, California.

www.ingramcontent.com/pod-product-compliance
Lightning Source LLC
Chambersburg PA
CBHW070111080526
44586CB00013B/1266